Praise for *Gospel Coach*

After leading hundreds of pastors and attending a few of their tragic funerals, Scott Thomas became burdened by God to create a gospel-centered coaching system to serve leaders. I am deeply thankful for all of t̲̅ ̲̅ ̲̅ nd excited to see him give this gift to th

̅ ̅ ̅ ̅ ̅ ·h,
rk

This is an outstanding book, filled ̲̅ ̲̅ d practical wisdom concerning the tr̲̅ ̲̅ ̲̅ God's people. The book reflects a solid understanding of Scripture and many years of pastoral ministry experience. It challenged and encouraged my own life, ministry, and walk with God. Highly recommended!

Wayne Grudem, research professor of theology and biblical studies,
Phoenix Seminary, Phoenix, Arizona

I've seen my friend Scott Thomas shepherd church leaders for years. Scott is aware of the issues leaders face in their personal, spiritual, and ministry lives. *Gospel Coach* is a practical and theologically rich book that will help produce healthy leaders to lead missional churches.

Ed Stetzer, president of LifeWay Research,
www.edstetzer.com

This book is biblical, theological, and extremely practical. It is Christ centered and gospel centered (though the two cannot be separated). This book is insightful and, at times, quite painful. The pain, however, is healing and redemptive. I like this book a lot. I will put it to good use for years to come.

Daniel L. Akin, president of Southeastern Baptist
Theological Seminary, Wake Forest, North Carolina

Filled with wisdom and insight, *Gospel Coach* gives a practical process for caring for the church of God by encouraging church leaders to focus on the right things. God's church needs healthy leaders who are not sidelined by the world's distractions. I encourage you to read it, digest it, and use it to help you fulfill God's call on your life.

Jonathan Falwell, pastor of Thomas Road
Baptist Church, Lynchburg, Virginia

In *Gospel Coach*, Scott Thomas and Tom Wood not only describe the practices necessary to be an effective shepherd/coach; they also explain how these practices must be (and can be) motivated by a heart that has been transformed by the gospel. I highly recommend it!

Steve Childers, president and CEO, Global Church Advancement, and
professor at Reformed Theological Seminary, Orlando, Florida

What a fantastic read and gold mine of resources Scott Thomas and Tom Wood have given us in *Gospel Coach*. As a young pastor, I would have tremendously benefited from the gospel-soaked wisdom and experience-birthed insights contained in these pages. The DNA of the gospel would have been woven more deeply into the organic life of our church. But now, twenty-five years later, I'm thankful to have a tool I can use to coach an emerging generation of impassioned church leaders who love the gospel of grace, the bride of Christ, and the kingdom of God. By all means, buy this book and encourage anyone with a heart for the church to do the same.

Scotty Smith, pastor for preaching,
Christ Community Church, Franklin, Tennessee

Gospel Coach takes the mystery out of coaching by sharing how women in ministry can have an intentional coaching relationship. Our female voice is needed for the advancement of the mission of the church, and *Gospel Coach* gives an easy-to-use tool for coaching others who follow in our footsteps.

Shari Thomas, founder and director of Parakaleo,
a ministry to church-planting spouses, and coauthor of Beyond
Duct Tape: Holding the Heart Together in a Life of Ministry

One of the great needs of our day is a "pastors shepherding pastors" movement. This book can equip and motivate pastors to become fully involved in this desperately needed ministry. It is gospel-saturated, biblically faithful, and realistically practical. Scott Thomas and Tom Wood have served the church well by providing us such a resource.

Tom Ascol, executive director of Founder's Ministries,
and pastor of Grace Baptist Church, Cape Coral, Florida

What *Gospel Coach* is really describing is intentional friendship and care, and we all need that. This book helps to ensure that friendship and care is centered on the gospel, addressed to the heart, and shepherds the person to Christ. I am definitely going to use it and enthusiastically encourage others to do the same.

Steve Timmis, author of Total Church,
director of Acts 29 Western Europe,
and founder of The Crowded House, Sheffield, UK

This tool has been essential in helping pastors and church planters to effectively lead their flocks and their families by developing a gospel-centered life plan.

George Ross, director of ONE8 Church Planting Network
and pastor of Lifepoint Church in Senatobia, Mississippi

GOSPEL COACH

SHEPHERDING LEADERS TO GLORIFY GOD

SCOTT THOMAS
AND TOM WOOD

ZONDERVAN®

ZONDERVAN.com/
AUTHORTRACKER
follow your favorite authors

We want to hear from you. Please send your comments about this book to us in care of zreview@zondervan.com. Thank you.

ZONDERVAN

Gospel Coach
Copyright © 2012 by Scott Thomas and Tom Wood

This title is also available as a Zondervan ebook.
Visit www.zondervan.com/ebooks.

Requests for information should be addressed to:

Zondervan, *Grand Rapids, Michigan* 49530

Library of Congress Cataloging-in-Publication Data

Thomas, Scott, 1959 Nov. 22-
    Gospel coach : shepherding leaders to glorify God / Scott Thomas and Tom Wood.
        p. cm.
    ISBN 978-0-310-49432-4 (softcover)
    1. Christian leadership. 2. Leadership — Religious aspects — Christianity.
    3. Clergy — Post-ordination training. I. Wood, Tom, 1957- II. Title.
    BV652.1.T476 2011
    253 — dc23   2011050692

Cover design: Patrick Mahoney
Interior design: Ben Fetterley and Matthew Van Zomeren

Printed in the United States of America

---

12 13 14 15 16 17 18 /DCI/ 21 20 19 18 17 16 15 14 13 12 11 10 9 8 7 6 5 4 3 2 1

To my sons, Derrin and Dustin.
I had the honor of coaching you
in all aspects of your life, but especially the gospel.
You helped me see more clearly
the love of our Father
and the joy we bring him by responding in faith.

— *Scott*

To Annie, Julie, and Amy, daughters of grace!
It gives this father great joy
to see his children grow up
and walk in the truth of the gospel.

— *Tom*

CONTENTS

PART 3: COACHING SESSIONS

APPENDIXES AND COACHING FORMS

FIGURES

TABLES

FOREWORD
BY DR. STEVE BROWN

THE CHURCH MAY BE BETTER than she seems, or at least not as bad as most observers think she is.

Don't get me wrong. As Augustine suggested, the church really is a prostitute and, at the same time, our mother. Just a cursory reading of church history will make any Christian wince. It's not a pretty picture. It never has been, and it won't be a pretty picture until Jesus comes back to clean up the mess.

But with that being said, just a cursory awareness of the church's work throughout its history will cause all but the most cynical among us (and I'm a cynical old preacher) to stand in astonishment at what God has done to glorify himself through some very sinful and human people. In fact, one gets the idea that the story would be even better if someone would put "legs" on the desire of most Christians to be "better than we are." Most of us in our finer moments want to love, serve, and glorify Christ more.

When asked about a list of problems facing the church of Jesus Christ in our time, almost everyone speaks about the need for holiness, obedience, biblical doctrine, solid theology, faithfulness, gospel clarity, cultural relevance, and a great variety of other pressing items. To question the "list" of what is needed would be the moral equivalent of opposing motherhood and apple pie. The needs of the church are indeed great, as we are all aware.

In fact, there are a great number of books that adequately define the problems of the church. I rise up and call the authors of those books blessed.

But sometimes one yearns for the practical and "doable." Practical and doable define this book. Scott Thomas and Tom Wood have asked and answered the questions about the problems in the church by asking, "What do we do now?" and "How do we do it?" They have presented gospel, biblical, and theological truth to answer those questions with so much clarity that it makes me want to stand up and sing the "Hallelujah Chorus."

If you think this is just another book written for church leaders, you are wrong. It *is* that—an amazingly helpful book for those of us who are called to lead and to come alongside one another to do kingdom work. But this book is so much more. It is a biblical model for all of us who are biblically defined as a "kingdom of priests" and who have a desire to see the church tuck in her skirt and run the race effectively and in a manner that will glorify the God we serve—the God who has loved us beyond our imagining.

Read and underline this book and give it to everybody you know who cares that the church be all she can be. Whoever you are, God has called you to be a "coach," and I commend this book to you to teach you how to do it.

> —**Steve Brown** is the founder and president of Key Life Network. He is a talk show host, the author of numerous books, a seminary professor at Reformed Theological Seminary, and a much-in-demand speaker.

PREFACE

GOSPEL COACH PROVIDES CHRISTIAN LEADERS a theological foundation and a practical system to develop and equip other leaders in the local church to make disciples and to shepherd them to glorify God and to effectively lead. While its subtitle suggests it is for leaders, it can be used to coach believers in all stages of their lives — men and women of all maturity levels and ages. Denominational or network leaders can gospel coach pastors or regional leaders. Pastors can gospel coach their elders, fellow staff members, and up-and-coming leaders. Elders can gospel coach small group leaders, and disciples can gospel coach other disciples. In fact, parents can gospel coach their children with the principles contained in this book.

Gospel Coach is a collaborative project between church planting leaders from two different arenas. Scott Thomas serves as the president of Acts 29 Network and an executive elder at Mars Hill Church in Seattle. Dr. Tom Wood is the president of Church Multiplication Ministries in Atlanta, Georgia. Both have pastored for over thirty years, have started churches of their own, and have coached pastors for many years. Both continue to serve in leadership roles as pastors in local congregations.

The content of this book is a shared effort that occurred with great joy and synergism. Scott did the heavy lifting of editing his work and combining it with Tom's writing and doctoral dissertation into one unified voice. Personal pronouns and illustrated stories will, for the most part, be referring to Scott. Any time a story or reference is not attributed to Scott, Tom's name will be found in parentheses to clarify.

When a book is written to describe a new approach, it often presumes that other approaches are inadequate or inaccurate. This is not our intent. We are grateful for other resources of coaching for leader development in the church, and we simply want to bring explicit emphasis to the gospel as the means for developing leaders to glorify God. The main difference between the gospel coach approach and other coaching approaches is that gospel coaches integrate knowing (head) with doing (hands) and being (heart). Though "doing" is important, coaching leaders only in external skills and techniques can bypass real heart issues. The gospel coach approach is grounded in the belief that from our being (in Christ) emanates our doing. We are created in Christ Jesus for doing good works (Ephesians 2:10). We seek to help church leaders to pay careful attention to themselves (being) and to pay careful attention to leading others (doing) in the church that Jesus obtained with his own blood (Acts 20:28).

We pray that *Gospel Coach* will give clarity to coaching and leading others by stirring up the gifts, passion, and calling on people's lives. We pray that it will help pastors and other Christian leaders to lovingly lead the flock of God as the Good Shepherd Jesus Christ led his flock to himself and into his mission for his glory. We pray, too, that a renewal of the church erupts through coaching that is preeminently gospel centered.

ACKNOWLEDGMENTS

SCOTT

I wish to thank the following people for their efforts in helping to create this system of "gospel coach":

Jeannie Thomas—for her unending support in whatever I do. For thirty years, she has joyfully sacrificed time with me for the greater kingdom to invest in the next generation of healthy, reproducing leaders in the church.

Mark Driscoll—for his ongoing sacrifice, generosity, and commitment to train young men to lead in the local church.

Adriel Ifland—for her commitment to coaching and for creatively brainstorming with me as I dreamed about coaching leaders.

Anthony Ianniciello—for leading his team to develop the website to facilitate coaching. He and Gabe Coyne took ideas I had and made them come alive.

Acts 29 coaches—for their sacrifice to coach other church planters by shepherding them to glorify God.

TOM

Thanks to all the men God has allowed me to coach this last decade. You made me a better coach. I learned more from you than you did from me. Thanks to Steve Brown, who was living and teaching the gospel long before it became fashionable! You gave me a clear picture of Jesus Christ, who loved me and gave himself for me! And finally, thanks to Rachel, my gospel coach for thirty-three years.

INTRODUCTION

WHILE I WAS SERVING AS THE LEAD PASTOR of a thriving church in Colorado, I made one of the worst decisions of my life. Because I no longer wanted to deal with a stubborn elder, one day I suddenly resigned. At the time, I felt that I didn't have anyone in my life with whom I could discuss this issue objectively before making my decision. There was no one to help me sort through my emotions and my heart issues and to guide me toward a godly response. I didn't have anyone to coach me. Today, if I had a chance to do it all over again, I would respond to that elder in a completely different way. And though we can't change the past, years later I did return and publicly apologize to the church for my decision. That experience led me to create the structure behind the gospel coach approach, a way of promoting healthy leaders and healthy churches that glorify God.

In Paul Stanley and Robert Clinton's helpful book, *Connecting: The Mentoring Relationships You Need to Succeed in Life,* they suggest that there are three intensive mentoring-type relationships: the discipler, the spiritual guide, and the coach.[1] They suggest that each different mentor style calls for more deliberate and specific interaction and works best when all three dynamics are fully present.

According to Stanley and Clinton, the *discipler* entails a relational process in which a more experienced follower of Christ shares with a new believer the commitment, understanding, and basic skills necessary to know and obey Jesus Christ. The discipler teaches and enables a person to apply the gospel. The *spiritual guide* is a godly, mature follower of Christ who shares knowledge, skills, and basic philosophy about what it means to increasingly realize Christlikeness in all areas of life. The primary contributions of a spiritual guide are accountability, decisions, insights concerning questions, commitments, and direction affecting spirituality (inner life motivations) and maturity (integrating truth with life). The discipler enables others in the basics of following Christ; a spiritual guide, according to the authors, will help you sort out your mixed motives and refocus on Christ when your competing time demands and desire for man's approval blur your priorities. The *coach*, according to Stanley and Clinton, provides motivation and imparts skills, encouragement, and application to meet a task or challenge. The coach provides observation, feedback, and evaluation based on personal experience as the teaching vehicle.

Stanley and Clinton conclude that mentoring works best when all three dynamics are fully present. Though we call our book *Gospel Coach*, we aren't focusing on just the "coaching" aspect that Stanley and Clinton highlight in their book. In *Gospel Coach*, we seek to integrate all three types of mentoring into one coaching relationship. The gospel coach serves a leader as a discipler, a spiritual guide, and a coach. Gospel coaches are both *grace givers* and *truth tellers*. The gospel coach relationship is a mentoring relationship, but one that allows for adaptation to serve the disciple in word and deed. Effective coaching is about friendship, but it is a unique type of friendship built on the gospel.

The gospel coach approach has seven core commitments:

1. to glorify God by shepherding leaders in a holistic manner with the gospel
2. to make the gospel of Jesus Christ the primary focus of every coaching session
3. to shepherd leaders' hearts for gospel transformation
4. to hold to the authority and sufficiency of Scripture
5. to equip leaders to exhibit gospel implications as image bearers of God
6. to promote the local church as the seat of ministry where community, mission, and the gospel exude out to the world

7. to coach church leaders to be qualified, gospel-empowered developers of other church leaders, producing healthy, disciple-making churches

Whenever I teach and train leaders using the material in this book, many leaders tell me how easy it really is to effectively coach others in a practical way. In the pages ahead, I want to present a fun, practical, gospel-centric way to care for the church of God by shepherding disciples to glorify God.

> Pay careful attention to yourselves and to all the flock, in which the Holy Spirit has made you overseers, to care for the church of God, which he obtained with his own blood.
>
> —Acts 20:28

PART 1

GOSPEL COACH
FOUNDATIONS

CHAPTER 1

WHY EVERY CHURCH LEADER NEEDS A COACH

EVERY CHURCH LEADER NEEDS A COACH. And every church leader needs to be coaching other leaders. Many years ago, I felt this conviction burning inside of me because I knew it was biblical truth — I just didn't have a good paradigm for how it would work! Now, after having formally and informally coached hundreds of pastors and trained thousands in this model of coaching, I am seeing an even greater need for a way of serving the needs of church leaders that will multiply the message of the gospel, encourage the health of leaders and churches, and promote the expansion of the church globally.

Ministry leaders tend to be the most underresourced members of the church, often receiving the least amount of support and attention. I often hear lay and vocational leaders in the church share that they feel uncared for, underresourced, undertrained, and unappreciated. Coaching ministry leaders is a key aspect to their ongoing effectiveness as shepherds of the Lord's flock. We believe coaching is necessary because it is a process of imparting encouragement and skills to a leader in order to fulfill their ministry role — something every leader needs — but it is done in the context of a gospel *friendship*.

Far too often, churches treat those serving in the church as a commodity. We adopt a consumeristic approach to our relationships, and we use people to get the ministry done. We believe there is a better, more biblical way to work with the people in our churches. Pastors and church leaders can engage other church leaders and volunteers in a personal, loving, and equipping manner, providing the tools necessary to help them fulfill God's calling on their lives to make disciples and glorify him. People do have an immense need to be useful, but no one likes to be used.

WHAT IS COACHING?

Business professionals and church leaders are now seeking out coaching relationships to deal with many of their personal and professional challenges. The term *coach* originally referred to a horse-drawn carriage, something that was designed for the purpose of transporting people and mail. These horse-drawn carriages were originally manufactured in the small Hungarian town of Kocs (pronounced "kotch") beginning in the fifteenth century.[1] The word became used in a symbolic sense around 1830 to refer to an instructor or trainer. It appears in some of the publications of Oxford University as a slang term for a tutor who "carries" a student through an exam. Later, this metaphorical use of the word as someone who "carries" another was used in the realm of athletic competition, beginning in 1861.[2]

Coaching, in its original intent, refers to the process of transporting an individual from one place to another. This can be applied to athletic endeavors, music, art, theater, acting, public speaking, and professional skill development. One can now obtain a coach for almost any endeavor they wish to pursue. The concept of "life coaching" can be traced back to a former college football coach-turned-motivational speaker in the late 1970s. The life coach was considered to be a unique professional relationship in which one talks with another individual, over a period of time, exploring how to more fully engage their life to live "on purpose."[3]

A few years ago, I [Tom] decided to join a health club and began the regimen of getting my body into a healthier condition. I visited a local club and was invited to walk around the facility to see the services they provided. After watching men and women work out on machines that I had never seen before, I realized that I would need a personal coach to show me the ropes.

Working with a coach taught me several things. First, I learned that I needed the trainer's knowledge to help me get the most out of each exercise I was doing. Second, I saw that I needed a coach to train me in a holistic approach that included my diet, my lifestyle, and my physical exercise. It was not enough to look at just one area of my life — all of these aspects were interconnected. Third, I realized that I needed his encouragement and motivation. Many times I remember him spurring me on, pushing me just a little further than I would normally go, using words like, "You can do this; keep going; don't stop yet!" In addition, I also discovered that I needed accountability. Many mornings, if I hadn't scheduled an appointment with my coach and prepaid for the time together, it is likely I would never have made it to the workout. My coach was able to help me measure my progress as well. We had a starting point and were able to assess and measure improvements as we went along. This coaching relationship was a key to my physical success.

Many church leaders experience trials and suffering, both in their ministry and in their personal lives. Some of these are health related; others come from family issues or marital problems. In addition to these personal struggles, church leaders feel the burden of the multitude of problems faced by those they care for, those in their oversight. These are real issues — cancer, loss of employment, abandonment by friends and fellow elders, serious financial setbacks — and they can end up devastating leaders for months, sometimes taking them out of the work of ministry altogether. The pain they feel is acute and ongoing.

Church leaders are not exempt from life's problems, and like others, they experience personal weakness, wrestling with doubts and losing their passion for God and for his mission. In addition, they often face supernatural spiritual attacks. The question that we need to ask ourselves is this: *Who is shepherding the shepherds?* Where do ministry leaders in the local church find their own pastoral care? Most church leaders have no idea where to turn to find help. Paul Stanley and Robert Clinton note the following:

Society today is rediscovering that the process of learning and maturing needs time and many kinds of relationships. The "self-made" man or woman is a myth and, though some claim it, few aspire to it. It leaves people relationally deficient and narrow-minded ...

A coach is particularly important when you step into a new responsibility or try to do something you have never done before. A coach is also helpful when you bog down in a responsibility.[4]

Many church leaders and pastors feel lonely, abandoned, and vulnerable, deeply desiring relationships where they can be real and honest with another person, but they are also fearful of safely sharing their heart's deepest concerns with members of their particular church body—even other leaders—so they frequently suffer in silence. Often, they fail to practice repentance or confession of their sin, and as a result, they are hampered in their ability to properly shepherd the flock they have been assigned to oversee. They are wounded, and the entire flock suffers when its shepherds are not healthy. Coaching other disciple-leaders is vital to the health of the leader and his family, as well as to the organization he is serving.

EFFECTIVENESS OF COACHING

Dallas Seminary professor Howard Hendricks once estimated that between 80 and 90 percent of leadership development is on-the-job training. This means that without on-the-job training, much of the work of training and equipping a leader is simply a waste of time. Those who participate in the fields of sports, education, business, medicine, the arts, fitness, and finances instinctively know this is true. In fact, if you were to take a moment to reflect on your own life and professional development, you will likely remember one or two people who had a large influence in shaping your thinking, abilities, career decisions, and possibly even character. I am indebted to my high school English and journalism teacher, Dave W. Robb, who "coached" me through some on-the-job training in the area of writing while I served as a columnist and editor of our school paper. His investment in my life has paid multiple dividends over the past thirty years. I also remember my high school principal, Warren "Wo"

Carere, who coached me "on the job" to lead the basketball team as its captain for two years. His investment in me was another turning point in my life.

Michael Jordan is arguably the greatest basketball player to ever play the game. But prior to Phil Jackson coming on the scene, Jordan's team won only 48 percent of their games and their team had no championships, even though Jordan often led the league in scoring. After Jackson became the head coach for the Chicago Bulls, they won 75 percent of their games and six championships. Michael Jordan always had great talent and natural ability, but coaching made a significant difference in helping him reach his full potential.

Much of our own experience in coaching leaders is in the area of church planting. The Southern Baptist Convention recently conducted research on six hundred church planters, and Dr. Ed Stetzer concluded, "Planters who met weekly with a mentor . . . led churches that were almost twice the size of those who had no mentor."[5] In a similar study by The Foursquare Church, they found that church planters who met monthly with a coach or mentor increased their baptisms by 150 percent and experienced a significant increase in worship attendance in contrast to those who lacked a coach or mentor.[6] While numerical growth in itself is not an accurate gauge of the effectiveness of coaching, it does provide a leading indicator, hinting at the difference coaching makes in the life of a leader.

BENEFITS OF COACHING

When I train leaders how to be gospel coaches, I always ask the participants why they believe it's important for church leaders to have a coach. Here are some of the most common responses:

- Coaching helps remind a leader of the gospel that shepherds need to be shepherded.
- Coaching exposes a leader's blind spots.
- Because leaders are capable of succumbing to sin's deception, coaching is preventative maintenance, a practical means for a leader to pay careful attention to one's self.
- The stakes for a church leader are high, and coaching can protect the flock from a leader's mistakes and bad decisions.

- Coaching models biblical community and discipleship.
- Coaching provides a prayer partner for a leader.
- Leaders can be prideful, and coaching helps a leader identify and fight arrogance.
- Leading can be lonely, and coaching brings encouragement to a leader.
- Coaching improves a leader's perspective and objectivity.
- Coaching facilitates a leader's growth and equipping.
- Coaching sharpens a leader's calling.
- Coaching is a means for intentional accountability and submission.
- Ministry is a difficult and complicated task, and coaching sharpens a leader's skills and abilities.
- Coaching provides a safe sounding board and a means to obtain advice from a fellow leader
- Coaching is fun, and it encourages friendship and provides affirmation for a leader's decisions.
- Coaching enables personal sanctification.
- Coaching protects family and marital health.

As you can see from the responses, the benefits of coaching are not only for the leader himself; coaching is also of great benefit to the church and to the community the leaders are serving and reaching.

Faithful leaders will make disciples, but great leaders focus on making other leaders. A leader doesn't learn to lead by attending a class or reading a book on leadership. A leader learns to lead best when he or she begins to lead others and is coached along the journey by a mentor. As the ministry leader is learning and applying the gospel in his or her own life, the followers will learn from what they see modeled in the life of their leader. They will be equipped and empowered by the gospel through the practical example and the visible fruit of that leader's life.

Gary Collins once made a bold statement about the importance of leadership development: "Good coaching is the key to producing good leaders. In changing times, to be a good leader you must be a good coach. And to be a good coach, you must recognize that coaching is a significant and increasingly emerging form of leadership and leadership training."[7] A church planting oversight team from a church I was working with once asked me (Tom) about my coaching relationship with their new planter. "Here's how I see my job as coach," I said. "It's to prepare him every week to be ready to play up to his personal best, as God has equipped and made him. He may never be an All-Pro-level pastor. I am not trying to coach him to be that level. But I can assist him in becoming someone in and through whom God can do miraculous things."

The key benefit of this type of coaching is *not* that it somehow produces the next all-star, celebrity leader. The benefit of gospel coaching is that it takes the message of the gospel—a message proclaiming that God takes weak and ordinary people and does great things through them to show off the surpassing greatness of Jesus Christ—and uses it to transform leaders and their churches so that they, in turn, will be used to transform the lives of others. Coaching isn't the secret to greatness; it's a proven means to facilitate gospel transformation in every area of a ministry leader's life *so that* he can effectively lead others in the mission of God through his local church.

WHY EVERY LEADER NEEDS A COACH

Many ministry leaders serving in churches find themselves overwhelmed by the challenging task of leading and ministering in a congregation. Being a church leader can be compared to herding cats, and it is far too normal for leaders, over time, to become disillusioned, distracted, and depressed. As a result, the ministry suffers and the leaders suffer, and the result is often an unhealthy church that has little or no gospel influence.

Every leader needs someone in his or her life who serves as a coach. After observing Christian leaders for thirty years, I (Scott) have compiled a list of twenty issues that I find Christian leaders hide from others, with the result that they often suffer alone. With only a couple of exceptions, I have experienced every one of these at some point in my life.

1. I'm really just average in my skills.
2. I'm often not sure what I'm supposed to be doing.

3. I have hidden emotional issues, some of which are derived from my relationship with my father and my mother.
4. I'm often motivated by self-glory.
5. I'm battling sin constantly (and losing occasionally).
6. I work way too much.
7. I have an inconsistent spiritual life.
8. People get on my nerves.
9. My marriage is average.
10. I'm not sure if I'm a good dad/mom/husband/wife.
11. I really don't find joy in my job.
12. I'm too young and inexperienced/my best days are behind me.
13. I'm really uncomfortable around unsaved people.
14. I don't have a close friend I can trust.
15. I rely on my position and guilt to get people to do things.
16. I make decisions without prayer or consulting others.
17. I waste my time on trivial matters.
18. I am often more concerned about myself than others.
19. I'm struggling financially.
20. I'm often tempted sexually.

At the heart of many of these problems are several things. Loneliness and isolation can become debilitating factors that negatively affect church leaders. Archibald Hart notes that the aloneness factor often leads to arrogance, which can lead to addiction and then adultery.[8] Another major reason for these problems is the reality of spiritual warfare, an issue that sometimes is ignored or minimized. Satan, the enemy of God, hates the church and does not want to see healthy, reproductive churches led by gospel-empowered people. Why should it surprise us to find Satan working to destroy the church by devouring ministry leaders and their families?

Though these and many other causes need to be addressed, our greatest concern in all of this is *a leader's heart*. Every human heart has a tendency toward dependence on its own ingenuity, natural ability, and fleshly effort. And church leaders are certainly not immune to this tendency. A very real and present danger in the life of every church leader is a growing coldness of heart, losing the vitality, pliability, and centeredness on God's grace that gives life and empowerment to all that we do.

In an attempt to help church leaders succeed in their personal and professional lives, some have introduced coaching systems that promise to help them be more productive, strategic, and effective in reaching goals and developing their leadership skills. The focus has typically been on competence through consulting and mentoring and on guiding him or her into a more desirable future. While these things are important in their right context, coaching of this type fails to address the fundamental issue for pastors and church leaders: *Who is shepherding my soul?* The truth is, you can pay someone $300 an hour to coach you in making decisions about budgets, bylaws, buildings, boards, and Bible studies. But even after finding solutions to these technical challenges, a leader can still feel miserable, living in a state of hopeless anxiety that is devoid of God's power and presence.

What leaders need is someone to shepherd their souls so that they, in turn, can lead others to the chief Shepherd, Jesus Christ. Coaching for church leaders looks less like corporate consulting and more like biblical shepherding. Every church leader needs someone to come alongside them to encourage, admonish, comfort, and help with words of truth drawn from Scripture and godly wisdom, grounded in the gracious saving work of Jesus Christ and presented in the context of trusting relationships.

BIBLICAL COACHING EXAMPLES

A seminary student asked me why we use the term *coaching* to describe our system for equipping leaders and making disciples. I explained it as just a term to characterize the transference of skills (doing), character (being), and knowledge (knowing) to another person in the same way Jesus, Barnabas, and Paul illustrated in the Bible. Augustine affirmed, "There is no better way of seeking truth than by the method of question and answer."[9] Coaching facilitates this dialogical interaction in an effective manner.

JESUS TO THE TWELVE
The best model of coaching people to change the world is Jesus Christ in his relationships with the twelve apostles. Jesus' three-year ministry with Peter, James, John, Andrew, Matthew, Bartholomew,

Judas, Philip, Thaddaeus, Simon the Zealot, James the son of Alphaeus, and Thomas provides a clear and compelling example of biblical coaching.

Jesus *knew* his disciples. He entered into a relationship with them and spent considerable time with them, particularly Peter, James, and John. He knew their strengths and weaknesses and related to them accordingly.

Jesus *fed* his disciples. He taught them and focused on their attitudes, motivations, and character. Jesus devoted his attention to the disciples' character growth and not necessarily on their goal setting, strategic planning, or even disciple-making skills. One would be hard-pressed to find ministry issues not addressed by Jesus.

Jesus *led* his disciples. He led them to relate to God and to be the type of men that God wanted them to be. Gunter Krallman writes, "Jesus concentrated his instruction more on those attitudes and spiritual principles which underlie and determine conduct, relationship building, skill application, and ministry performance."[10] Jesus led the Twelve out in pairs on their first mission endeavor (Matthew 10:5 – 14; Mark 6:7 – 13; Luke 9:1 – 6). He gave them specific instructions on what they were to do and where they were to go. He coached them by leading them to minister effectively, and then he followed up with them after their first ministry experience.

Jesus *protected* his disciples. He did this by addressing weaknesses and sins, paying particular attention to their demonstration of humility. He rebuked their unbelief and reconciled with them when they failed (John 20:24 – 29; 21:15 – 19).

BARNABAS TO PAUL

Barnabas is another example of coaching found in the New Testament. Barnabas was called "Son of Encouragement" because he was generous with his time and possessions. It was Barnabas who introduced Saul (later named Paul) to the apostles.

Gospel coaches are encouragers. Coaches recognize the gifts and abilities that God has placed within the disciple-leader and encourage their use and development. Barnabas recognized the calling of God on Paul's life and encouraged him by pastoring, teaching, and evangelizing together with him.

PAUL TO TIMOTHY

Paul was a developer of leaders. He appears to be a dominant, task-oriented, and risk-taking leader. Yet, he knew the value of relationship in coaching younger leaders. Throughout his epistles he names almost eighty people with whom he shared personal relationships—most notable was Timothy. Paul forged a unique relationship with Timothy, referring to him as (1) "a son with a father" (Philippians 2:22), (2) "my true child in the faith" (1 Timothy 1:2), and (3) "my beloved child" (2 Timothy 1:2).

Paul wrote, "Be imitators of me, as I am of Christ" (1 Corinthians 11:1) and "What you have learned and received and heard and seen in me—practice these things, and the God of peace will be with you" (Philippians 4:9). Paul focused his development of Timothy in three main aspects: personal (1 Timothy 3:1–13; 2 Timothy 2:1; Titus 1–2), missional (1 Timothy 5:17; 2 Timothy 4:2, 5), and spiritual (2 Timothy 3:14–17; Titus 1:9). Paul was deeply interested in the development of Timothy's whole life, and he sought to encourage, equip, and empower him.

PAUL TO TITUS

The maturation and development of Titus's life is yet another beautiful illustration of how coaching can produce quality leaders and be an effective form of leadership training. Coaching is a reproductive process of training leaders to develop others (2 Timothy 2:2).

Notice the leadership development of Titus:

1. Titus was a friend who encouraged Paul (2 Corinthians 7:6). When Paul was downcast, Titus's arrival brought comfort and encouragement.
2. Titus was intrigued by the work of the ministry of the Macedonians (2 Corinthians 7:13). The spirit of Titus was refreshed by the work of the Macedonians that he observed for himself firsthand.
3. Titus was a faithful worker carrying out the wishes of Paul (2 Corinthians 8:6; 12:17). Paul sent Titus on ministry errands that he faithfully completed.

4. Titus developed a heart for the ministry and initiated ministry on his own (2 Corinthians 8:16–17). God put into the heart of Titus the same earnest care that Paul had for the ministry, and Titus began to act on his own initiative.
5. Titus was a proven minister (2 Corinthians 8:23). Paul referred to Titus as his partner and fellow worker for the benefit of the Macedonian church.
6. Titus became the senior overseer to appoint elders throughout the island of Crete. His proven faithfulness and calling allowed him to pioneer works in this hostile environment (Titus 1:4–5).

DECIDING WHO TO COACH

Jesus handpicked twelve men to be his disciples (Mark 3:13–19; Luke 6:13–16). Barnabas traveled to Tarsus in search of Paul (Acts 11:19–26). Paul chose Timothy with recommendations from the church at Lystra (Acts 16:1–3). How will you decide whom to coach? I believe every person can coach at least four people. This requires investing approximately two hours a week (5 percent of a forty-hour work week) into coaching each person twice a month for one hour. Each of us can only coach a limited number of people, so it requires careful discernment to determine whom God is calling you to coach. I personally believe that it is the best use of kingdom resources and your time to select people who can eventually coach others. When Paul released Timothy from his direct care, he told him to focus on developing other leaders: "You then, my child, be strengthened by the grace that is in Christ Jesus, and what you have heard from me in the presence of many witnesses entrust to faithful men *who will be able to teach others also*" (2 Timothy 2:1–2, emphasis added).

In addition, because of the deep personal, relational, and spiritual connection formed in the coaching relationship, we strongly discourage coaching someone of the opposite gender. Though there may be rare situations where this is permissible (a married couple or a relative or family member), it is not a model we would advocate or support.

THE EXTENT OF GOSPEL COACHING

Gospel coaching can be implemented in a number of relational applications (see Figure 1):

- denominational or network leader to pastor
- pastor to pastor
- pastor to fellow elders
- elders to community group leaders
- community group leaders to group participants
- disciples to disciples
- parents to children

I coach other network leaders, pastors in Acts 29 and in Mars Hill Church, as well as my two sons (ages twenty-three and nineteen). It might surprise you to see the parent/child relationship included in the list of possible coaching relationships, but I have found that the gospel coach model of training leaders is helpful in teaching and training children. Not long ago, my oldest son was trying to make a decision, and he walked into my bedroom and asked me to coach

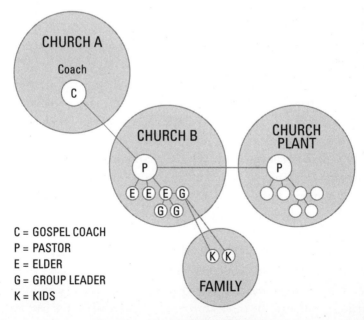

Figure 1: Extent of Gospel Coaching

him. At times, my focus in coaching my sons is on protecting them—sharing wisdom and warning them against many of the temptations and challenges of life. But I also spend much of my time coaching them on how to make decisions on their own—decisions based on truth, experience, and wisdom. They respond more quickly when I spend time with them in this way instead of when I simply tell them what to do or give them my opinion.

WHAT IS GOSPEL COACHING?

As we will explain in the chapters that follow, gospel coaching is a means to glorifying God through Spirit filled, cross-centered relationships that produce gospel-centered identity in Christ, worship, unity with a community of believers, and mission to people of all nations. It is an intentional relationship for working out the implications of the gospel in a person's life.

For example, a gospel coach must seek to understand the personal life of a disciple. Let's say that the person being coached has expressed a need for a new vehicle. Instead of just problem solving the best way of obtaining that new car, a gospel coach will seek to probe the deeper issues of the heart—their motivation, their spiritual idols, the unseen consequences that might come from obtaining a new vehicle.

In another example, a coach might seek to help a person manage their time with new skills and principles of time management, perhaps utilizing a resource such as David Allen's *Getting Things Done*.[11] But a gospel coach would go beyond mere assistance in managing time or skill development by lovingly questioning their priorities and exposing them in light of Scripture, leading them to make decisions that are based on the truth revealed in the gospel, and then protecting them by either confronting their decision or holding them accountable to it.

As indicated below (Figure 2), gospel coaching is a relationship-based process of communicating the message of the gospel from a coach to a disciple-leader (pictured as words spoken into a bullhorn), projected through the three aspects of a person's life—the personal, spiritual, and missional. The outcome of this process is a Spirit-filled

Figure 2: Gospel Coaching Main Illustration

disciple who worships God with every area of his life, has his identity in Christ, is truly united in gospel community, and is on a mission to the people of all nations. And this happens *through* a shepherding process in which a person is known, fed, led, and protected by their gospel coach.

I coached basketball and football for about twenty years. On only a few occasions was I asked by an athlete to evaluate his progress. Yet I watched every move every player made and then continually provided instruction, correction, and encouragement where applicable. I pulled players off the court and field during the game when their actions were not progressing, and I issued up-close and personal instruction. In practice, we reinforced those desired skills specific to each player. I saw young men transform into highly productive athletes who helped their teams win championships while they excelled personally. Gospel coaching is not much different. A coach observes a disciple, listens carefully, and offers feedback to help them to lead others in this glorious mission of Jesus Christ.

Gospel coaching is this type of intentional relationship, skillfully caring for others in a way that is guided by four ancient principles of shepherding:

1. know the sheep
2. feed the sheep
3. lead the sheep
4. protect the sheep

A gospel coach inquires about the personal, spiritual, and missional aspects of a ministry leader's life in a loving, yet focused manner. A coach also probes the heart motivation of a church leader for compulsive unbelief or selfish impulses. He lovingly looks for evidences of disobedience and sin and leads the individual back to the gospel through repentance and faith. Coaching provides the means of combining effective discipleship with leadership training, and it leads to three key benefits:

1. A coach provides feedback, correction, and guidance for pending decisions.
2. A coach provides counsel, admonishment, and encouragement for challenges.
3. A coach provides steps of action and strategies for following God's calling.

A gospel coach doesn't sit passively awaiting an invitation to educate and evaluate. He gets to know the life of the disciple-leader, feeds them appropriate truth, leads them to progress in their calling by God, and then protects them through encouragement and rebuke. Good coaching involves personally observing the disciple in life and action, and instructing for the benefit of the disciple.

Most importantly, though, effective coaching only functions properly with a thorough understanding of the gospel, of its central role in the life of a believer, and of its ongoing work to produce gospel transformation, healthy leaders, and theologically rich churches reproducing for the glory of God and the good of the mission of Jesus Christ. If the gospel is not at work in the life of church leaders, then it is highly unlikely it will be at work in the life of the church.

CHAPTER 2

WHY EVERY CHURCH LEADER NEEDS THE GOSPEL

MANY YEARS AGO, a pastor of a church in New England faced power struggles over his salary and his leadership style. A few parents were disillusioned by the way he rebuked one young boy's sinful behavior. Several church members accused him of not loving the people because his gifts were predominantly in the area of preaching and teaching. They felt he lacked compassion and understanding. All of this, despite the fact that this pastor had been instrumental in leading a revival that had impacted thousands of people and had lasted for several years. As the situation worsened, a large opposition group formed. When this pastor refused to allow unbelievers to join the membership of the church, the church fired him from his pastorate. He was forty-six years old and had faithfully served the people in that community for twenty-three years. Suddenly, he was unemployed, treated like an outcast by his church members.

It took almost 150 years for that same church to repent of their actions toward their ousted pastor. His name, as you may know, is Jonathan Edwards—the pastor and theologian most commonly associated with the First Great Awakening in America, a time of unprecedented spiritual fervor and the display of many mighty works of God.[1] I mention Edwards to highlight that, while we often remember the high points of ministry success, the truth is that much of ministry involves an array of widely different experiences — times of both success and failure, joy and great struggle. Church leaders deal with all of this as they minister to people.

The stress of leading a church along with the responsibility of trying to maintain an exemplary family can often be overwhelming. The *New York Times* offers this discouraging report:

> The findings have surfaced with ominous regularity over the last few years, and with little notice: Members of the clergy now suffer from obesity, hypertension, and depression at rates higher than most Americans. In the last decade, their use of antidepressants has risen, while their life expectancy has fallen. Many would change jobs if they could.[2]

As we have begun to recognize, church leaders are not immune to sin's effects on their personal, spiritual, and missional lives. They regularly admit that ministry takes a difficult toll on their family, their marriage, and their health. And when church leaders suffer, the church itself suffers. David Olson writes that "the American church is in crisis" and cites research that shows that 77 percent of Americans "do not have a consistent, life-giving connection with a local church."[3] The church in America appears to have lost much of its theology, its spiritual fervor, its mission, and its worship of God and is no longer a community of Spirit-filled disciples who are unified for the common good of bringing glory to God.

So how are churches responding to the problem of rising stress among their leaders?

ATTEMPTS TO SOLVE THE STRESS OF CHURCH LEADERSHIP ISSUES

Christian Smith, professor of sociology and director of the Center for the Study of Religion and Society at the University of Notre Dame, oversees a continuing study of the religious beliefs of teenagers called the National Study of Youth and Religion. After interviewing hundreds of teens about religion, God, faith, prayer, and other spiritual practices, Smith and his colleagues have identified the common beliefs that the average teenager holds:

1. A God exists who created and ordered the world and watches over human life on earth.
2. God wants people to be good, nice, and fair to each other, as taught in the Bible and by most world religions.
3. The central goal of life is to be happy and to feel good about oneself.
4. God does not need to be particularly involved in one's life except when God is needed to resolve a problem.
5. Good people go to heaven when they die.[4]

Smith has termed this system of beliefs "Moralistic Therapeutic Deism" (MTD). He clarifies that MTD is not an official religion but that it is simply a colonizing of many established religious traditions and congregations in the United States. The implication of all this is that the philosophies of MTD are dominating our churches, pulpits, books, and counseling and coaching sessions.

We believe that this reliance on moralism, therapeutic methodology, and a deistic understanding of God is commonly taught as the solution to many of the problems that the church faces—including the common struggles of most church leaders. Let's look at how these three aspects—moralism, therapy, and deism—betray a lack of understanding of the gospel of God's grace.

MORALISM—DO GOOD

Moralism is the belief that the Christian life can be reduced to improvements in behavior. The moralistic approach to life believes that central to living a good and happy life is being a good, moral person. This means being nice, kind, pleasant, respectful, and responsible; working on self-improvement; taking care of one's health; and doing one's best to be successful.

While many leaders may teach and believe they are justified by God's grace, they effectively deny that same grace by their efforts at being a godly leader. They rely on their own moral ability or on the way other people perceive them as good, moral people; thus, they are blind to their own sin. They trust in themselves or in the faulty judgment of others rather than in the grace of God, the cross of Christ, and the empowerment of the Holy Spirit. This type of leader often shames his family and the people he is leading into doing better and deals harshly with those who fail to perform to the level of acceptable behavior.

The gospel tells us that our standard for morality is Jesus Christ and that we only attain his perfect morality through his righteous imputation—we are declared righteous on the merits of Christ alone (Romans 4:3–8). As Tim Keller states, "I am more sinful and flawed than I ever dared believe. I am more accepted and loved than I ever dared hope."[5] A Christian leader who neglects the importance of the gospel relies instead on systems and structures that offer techniques for living a good life. Moralism leads to methods of behavior modification where we seek to change what we do without addressing who we are as sinful people. Moralism does not help us gain favor with God or ease our pressure. In fact, those who rely on systems or structures for living a moral life or managing their sin are neglecting the gospel of Christ.

THERAPY — SMILE AND BE HAPPY

Therapy is the belief that adherents enjoy psychological benefits by participating in something good. This is not a religion of repentance from sin or of living as a servant of a sovereign God. Rather, therapy encourages us to pursue the goal of feeling good, happy, secure, and at peace with the world. It seeks to attain a state of subjective well-being by resolving problems and avoiding conflict with people. It's about doing good things *so that you feel good about yourself.*

There is a dangerously fine line between serving God and serving ourselves. Ministry leaders may tend to overuse their "speaking for God" attitude to encourage followers to find their own happiness, since, as they say, "God wants you happy." Others may encourage disciples to apply "easy-to-follow steps to personal wholeness." Some leaders may lean toward the "be nice and smile" solution, ignoring the effects of sin. A person who embraces the therapeutic mind-set often focuses on the positives and avoids conflict at all costs—even if it involves compromising principles or the clear teaching of Scripture.

Many well-meaning Christian leaders offer therapeutic solutions to the problems we face. They often suggest that we simply need new hobbies or retreats or routines. One church leader said in an article that his best way of dealing with ministry stress is to listen to soothing music, hang out with some good friends, get a massage, and shoot his guns. Another leader said, "I take mental holidays while I am at church during the week." Still another said, "I have a note card that I wrote to myself that I stuck inside my desk. It simply says, 'Lighten up and smile.'"[6] These are all different ways of dealing with stress, and each takes a different approach to ignoring the root problems in the heart. I seriously doubt that a note card encouraging me to lighten up and smile will be of any benefit when a family member gets cancer or I'm counseling a friend who has just lost a child. Sadly, much of the "advice" given out by church leaders today is unbiblical. With our churches filled with leaders who believe these things, is it any wonder that Moralistic Therapeutic Deism is thriving in the church?

Deism—Be There If I Need You

Deism is the belief that there is a God who exists, who created the world, but who is now uninvolved in the affairs of life. God exists, but he basically leaves us alone. At a practical level, deism conceives of God as a Divine Butler who waits for us to call on him to intervene in times of great need or as a Cosmic Genie who exists to grant our wishes. If our plans and goals do not succeed as we expect, God gets the blame for our disappointment and pain.

A leader leaning into this belief in deism does not rest in the biblical teaching that God is sovereign and that all things in life happen for God's purposes, so he is prone to get a consultant or to seek additional education that will help him fix the problems he faces. He has a tendency to spend most of his time working on the superficial structures of his life and to align his leadership philosophy with maxims and pragmatic, quick-fix ideals. He adapts quickly to methods that are good and that work rather than adopting principles that guide.

PROBLEMS IN LIFE COACHING METHODS

At its core, Moralistic Therapeutic Deism is based on a humanistic, man-centered way of seeing our problems. And it offers solutions that we can manage and accomplish in our own strength and wisdom, without depending on God. In this sense, it is directly opposed to the gospel of God's grace, which declares us dead in our sins, desperately in need of salvation that only God can provide through the atoning, all-sufficient work of Jesus Christ. But MTD is not the only evidence of humanistic thinking in the church today. Much of the contemporary coaching movement that seeks to guide and equip leaders in the church and business world is also marked by this type of thinking.

One of the best-known attempts at solving the problem of leadership in the church is the "life coaching" movement. Many of the foundational principles and practices of life coaching are founded on secular, humanistic theories. In fact, the life coaching movement has its roots in humanistic principles espoused by Carl Rogers, Abraham Maslow,[7] Carl Jung,[8] Alfred Adler,[9] and Milton Erickson.[10]

Carl Rogers's 1951 book *Client-Centered Therapy* defines counseling and therapy as a relationship in which the client is assumed to have the ability to change and grow by a therapeutic alliance formed between the clinician and the client. This alliance evolved from a safe, confidential space that grants the client what Rogers calls "unconditional positive regard"—blanket acceptance and support of a person regardless of what the person says or does. It was this shift in perspective toward the person being helped that allowed for the development of what is today known as life coaching. Instead of a relationship defined by biblical concepts of love, accountability to God, and covenantal obligations and responsibilities, we have shifted to a coaching and counseling model that affirms all of our life choices. Humanism places an emphasis on subjective experience and human potential. In fact, Carl Rogers taught that people could solve their own problems if given the freedom to self-actualize. He believed that humans are morally good and that personal experience is the highest authority to guide us in life.

The life coaching movement often targets people who are seeking personal evolution and fulfillment, and it assists people by working toward the client's improved outcomes or achievements. At first glance, this may not sound all that bad, but upon closer examination we find that it is rooted in humanistic psychology. The main focus of most life coaching today is not *pathology*—a thorough examination of the nature of our problems and their causes, processes, development, and consequences. Rather, humanism is focused on *behavioral change* through increased awareness and choices to allow for desired future results and solutions to current "problems in living."[11] In other words, much of life coaching is less concerned with issues of sin, rebellion against God, and our need for a Savior; it is about helping us achieve our self-determined goals in life, enabling us to seek happiness in fulfilling our personal desires.

POTENTIAL PROBLEMS IN CHRISTIAN COACHING

Following the lead of the life coaching movement, some Christian coaching contributors, perhaps unknowingly, have drawn some of their theories and practices from Carl Rogers and other humanistic theoreticians. Unfortunately, many of those theories are based on the assumption that the client is basically good and that the answers to the maladies of life are found by "looking inside" and focusing on our desires. Rogers taught that man is good and that corruption enters our lives from the outside. Larry Crabb suggests Rogers believed that through a process of self-actualization,[12] man would become all that he is able to become.[13] Rogers advocated a nondirective, client-centered therapy (CCT) approach to solving personal problems in which the therapist/coach *deliberately avoids* directing or instructing the client in a particular way—even if he feels it can help the client. According to this approach, the answers to a client's questions are already there inside him, and so the coach must reflect the client back to himself through asking questions and mirroring back to the client their own statements, all without imposing their own ideas. Rogers suggested that one of the goals of coaching was to move the person toward becoming autonomous, gradually choosing the goals toward which he wanted to move.[14]

Some of the humanistic coaching methodologies utilized by Christian coaches are seemingly antithetical to their own teaching about other biblical concepts.[15] Perhaps stemming from a lack of good gospel-centered resources for coaching, much of the contemporary Christian coaching movement seems to suffer from an unhealthy reliance on Rogerian therapeutic methods. As churches attempt to provide coaching for church planters, pastors, and Christian leaders, it is necessary to realize that some Christian authors are drawing from a source of coaching information that may be devoid of the message and implications of the gospel.

As an example of this approach, many Christian coaches use the principles found in John Whitmore's book *Coaching for Performance*. Whitmore acknowledges that he developed his own theory and practice of coaching by following the humanistic psychology taught by Abraham Maslow, a contemporary of Carl Rogers, both of whom contributed to the "self-actualizing" movement. Whitmore believed that to "get the best out of people, we have to believe the best is in there" and he based his coaching model on this assumption—the inherent goodness of people.[16] One Christian coaching author follows this line of thinking, arguing that "coaching focuses on promoting discovery... By helping you focus on the untapped potential within you, a coach can guide you to discover that potential and what needs to be done."[17] Both of these approaches wrongly assume that by simply discovering one's potential, problems can be solved. But this is a wrong assumption that is based on the notion that people are inherently good, that rather than being inherently selfish they are simply in need of self-discovery. In contrast, we contend that *any* approach that relies on a client-centered coaching approach, even if it flies under the banner of being Christ centered, is fundamentally flawed.

The Scriptures clearly reject the presupposition of our moral goodness, insisting that the effects of the fall stemming from human disobedience and rebellion against our Creator are much worse than we dare believe. The apostle Paul wrote:

> I know that nothing good dwells in me, that is, in my flesh. For I have the desire to do what is right, but not the ability to carry it out. For I do not do the good I want, but the evil I do not want is what I keep on doing. Now if I do what I do not want, it is no longer I who do it, but sin that dwells within me.
>
> —Romans 7:18–20

We often advise people to merely "follow your heart." Yet the prophet Jeremiah informs us that "the heart is deceitful above all things, and desperately sick; who can understand it?" (Jeremiah 17:9). In other words, the Bible teaches that we are so prone to self-deception that we may not even know when we are lying to ourselves, much less to a person coaching us! Even as coaches, we must acknowledge that we are prone to this self-deception. Ephesians 2:1 states that as sinners, we are "dead in . . . trespasses and sins." In verse 3, we learn that the sinner actively practices evil and is enslaved to sin because his natural desire is to gratify the cravings of his sinful nature and follow its desires and thoughts, not the desires of God. As he "coached" his young disciple and fellow leader Timothy, the apostle Paul warned him that that there is a trap that can take a person captive by Satan "to do his will" (2 Timothy 2:26). Without the intervening work of Christ in our lives, we all fall into this trap. We have no other choice; we are slaves to our sinful desires.

To experience their full God-ordained potential, a Christian leader must first recognize that he or she is a forgiven sinner made righteous entirely through Jesus Christ and not through their own merit or ability. Transformation occurs as Christians appropriate the gospel and live by faith in what God declares true in Jesus. Those who have been transformed by the power of this message recognize that every wrong action, thought, or emotion is fundamentally a form of unbelief in the gospel, in what it declares to be true.

Though a person can believe the message of the gospel, functionally we often reveal a deeper, heart-level belief that our power, approval, comfort, and security are more worthy of pursuit than God. Since Jesus Christ is the only way that God has provided for us to be saved, we sin when we find our meaning and worth in anything other than our identity in Christ. This sin is a form of idolatry, a refusal to believe the good news that God has saved us in Jesus alone, instead looking to and relying on someone or something to give to us what only God can give. David Powlison explains this connection between biblical idolatry, sin, and our hearts:

> Has something or someone besides Jesus Christ taken title to your heart's trust, preoccupation, loyalty, service, fear, and

delight? It is a question bearing on the immediate motivation for one's behavior, thoughts, and feelings. In the Bible's conceptualization, the motivation question is the lordship question. Who or what "rules" my behavior, the Lord or a substitute?[18]

Whereas the humanistic approach to coaching tells us that the problem we face is "out there" and the solution we need is inside of us, the gospel teaches us the exact opposite, namely, that the problem is really inside the heart and mind and the answer to our problem is outside of us—not in our work or effort—but in Christ alone. The gospel is the ultimate solution for every problem we face, and the answer is obviously not something we find inside of us. The power of the gospel comes when we look away from ourselves, relying on Jesus. As we trust in Jesus and his work on our behalf, we receive the supernatural power of God through the gracious gift of his Spirit.

In light of this, Christian coaching methodology that fails to begin with the gospel will often end up relying on technique-oriented methods that are derived from a humanistic foundation. Henri Nouwen offered this insightful critique of the state of most Christian leadership today:

> Few ministers and priests think theologically. Most of them have been educated in a climate in which the behavioral sciences, such as psychology and sociology, so dominated the educational milieu that little true theology was being learned. Most Christian leaders today raise psychological and sociological questions even though they frame them in scriptural terms. Real theological thinking, which is thinking with the mind of Christ, is hard to find in the practice of ministry. Without solid theological reflection, future leaders will be little more than pseudo-psychologists … They will think of themselves as enablers, facilitators, role models, father or mother figures, big brothers or big sisters, and so on, and thus join the countless men and women who make a living by trying to help their fellow human beings to cope with the stresses and strains of everyday living. But that has little to do with Christian leadership.[19]

In light of this systemic problem in the leadership of the church, we believe there is a great need to recover a means of coaching and

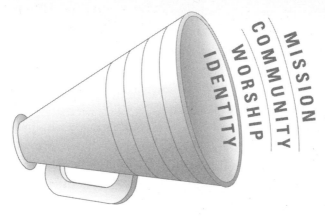

Figure 3: Gospel Coaching Outcomes

counseling others in the gospel, by the gospel, through the gospel, for the sake of Christ. The illustration above (Figure 3) shows us how the power of the gospel, when communicated into the life of the disciple-leader in a coaching context, will produce a disciple who has his identity rooted deeply in Christ as a child of God; is worshiping God with his heart, soul, spirit and might; is united with a gospel community; and is on mission to all people as a herald of the good news of Jesus. As the gospel goes into disciple-leaders, the "message" that is heard is a Spirit-filled follower of Jesus, living for the glory of God.

THE GOSPEL STORY

We are persuaded that the gospel must be the central foundation for effective, God-honoring biblical coaching. It is imperative, therefore, that we know what the gospel is and how it informs our practices. Terms like justification, adoption, sanctification, and sin are often clearly defined in several historical church documents, creeds, and confessions of the church. But there are surprisingly few classical definitions of the gospel. And there is a reason for this. Some have attempted to distill the deep truths of the gospel into terms or laws (the "four spiritual laws," for example) or have tried to visually illustrate the message by means of a bridge. Others summarize the main points with headings like God, Sin, Christ, and Faith, or by giving the high points of the story arc of the Bible. This approach communicates the gospel through movements in redemptive history and is often summarized by creation, sin, and redemption or by creation, fall, rescue, and restoration. In truth, the gospel is more of a story than a simple definition. In order to really grasp the gospel message, you have to immerse yourself in the narratives of the Bible, because transforming faith is more than just a statement that we accept; it is something that connects with both our minds and our hearts. It is a true story, rich with drama, action, and eternal significance.

Theologian J. I. Packer has written this about the gospel:

> What was this good news that Paul preached? It was the news about Jesus of Nazareth. It was news of the incarnation, the atonement, and the kingdom—the cradle, the cross, and the crown—of the Son of God. It was news of how God "glorified his servant Jesus" (Acts 3:13) by making him Christ, the world's long awaited "Leader and Savior" (Acts 5:31).[20]

The gospel is God's good news. The apostle Paul writes:

> Now I would remind you, brothers, of the gospel I preached to you, which you received, in which you stand, and by which you are being saved, if you hold fast to the word I preached to you—unless you believed in vain.
>
> For I delivered to you as of first importance what I also received: that Christ died for our sins in accordance with the Scriptures, that he was buried, that he was raised on the third day in accordance with the Scriptures ...
>
> —1 Corinthians 15:1–4

The gospel is God's good news about Jesus Christ. He is the central message of the gospel, and it is by hearing about what he has done (the gospel) and turning from our sinful rebellion (repentance) to trust in his work on our behalf (faith) that we are saved and can finally begin to understand the purpose for our lives. Because the gospel fundamentally changes our self-understanding and our perspective on life, it is the appropriate place to start when coaching others.

The message of the gospel is shallow enough for a child to wade in and yet deep enough to drown an elephant, and to grasp it we suggest following the summary of the gospel story through the four narrative acts of creation, fall, redemption, and restoration. As each act of the drama unfolds, it's important to keep in mind that the gospel is first and foremost *God's story*. Though it has important implications for our lives today, it is a story written and conceived by God himself. It describes how his created beings committed cosmic treason against his just and loving rule, and how he took the loving initiative to rescue his people out of their rebellion and from the consequences of our folly, guilt, and certain death. The full story of the gospel communicates the compelling truth about God, what he requires of us, and what he has done for us. It tells us the truth — about our world, about who we really are, and about our destiny.

CREATION: HOW IT ALL BEGAN

In the beginning, God created everything that exists — time, darkness, and light; the sun, moon, and stars; the earth and all its plants, animals, and people. The story of the gospel begins with a personal, eternally self-existent God. God is the originator of everything. He made time and space. He maintains everything, moment by moment, and all that exists currently is because of his will and desire. Through God's simple act of speaking, everything that exists came into existence for the purpose of glorifying God and his name.

The Bible tells us that God made all things. He made them good and beautiful, and he made them for a reason. Nothing is random or left to chance. God is omnipresent (existing everywhere), omniscient (knowing everything there is to know), and omnipotent (all-powerful). This teaching about the nature and character of God is an important gospel truth that often needs to be reinforced in the coaching relationship.

The first act of the gospel story tells us that Adam and Eve, our first parents, were made in the image of God to love, worship, and find their ultimate joy in God. The Westminster Catechism summarizes this teaching in its answer to the first question:

Q: What is the chief end of man?
A: Man's chief end is to glorify God, and to enjoy
   him forever.

Not only is God the source of all that exists in the material world; he is also the source of all meaning and purpose. He is the source of all joy and completeness. As created beings, we are made to worship and find our wholeness in him alone.

God placed our first parents in the Garden of Eden — a place of perfection and beauty — to rule it and to work it. They were created to love one other as one flesh and to live as worshipers of their Maker: "By God's design, all of creation was in harmony and was exactly the way it was supposed to be. During this time there was no pain, suffering, sickness, or death. There was complete love, acceptance, and intimacy between God and man, between Adam and Eve, and throughout creation."[21] The Bible tells us that this was the way God wanted it to be: "God saw everything that he made, and behold, it was very good" (Genesis 1:31).

God told Adam that he had complete freedom to live in Eden, with one small exception. God said to Adam that he was free to eat from any tree in the garden, but he was commanded to not eat from a particular tree located in the center of the garden: "Of the tree of the knowledge of good and evil you shall not eat, for in the day that you eat of it you shall surely die" (Genesis 2:17). In essence, God said to Adam, "Obey me, and you will live; disobey me, and you will die." Given the great freedom that God had given to Adam, this one request may seem like a rather inconsequential command. But God knew that it was a test and that in Adam's decision to obey or disobey this command, Adam held the destiny of the entire creation in his hands, including the future of those who would follow him, his descendants. All of us are included in the choices made by our first father, Adam, and we all live with the consequences of his decision.

THE FALL: WHAT WENT WRONG

Any great epic will also have an element of conflict, and the disastrous conflict of the gospel story is of cosmic proportions. The Bible gives significant emphasis to this event because it frames the drama that unfolds in the rest of the story. The biblical book of Genesis offers us unique insight into why our world, our relationships, and our spiritual lives are such a mess today. To put it simply, if we want to understand the "good" news of the gospel, we must first understand the "bad" news — the tragic fall of the human race through disobedience into rebellion and death.

Adam and Eve, the first human beings, lived full, meaningful, love-filled lives in a perfect world. But the world of the garden was not completely free from temptation. In the garden there was a serpent, a fallen, created angelic being known as Satan, who had rebelled against God and was intent on leading God's image bearers into following him in his evil and rebellion. Using craftiness and subtle deception, the serpent whispered into their hearts, tempting them to doubt God's clear commands and promises and put their trust in their own wisdom and the word of the serpent. Satan tempted Adam and Eve with unbelief, prompting them to question God's word: "Did God actually say, 'You shall not eat of any tree in the garden'?" (Genesis 3:1). He tempted them to consider what life could be like if they disowned their dependence on their Creator. Satan invited them to determine for themselves what was right and wrong, luring them to live in autonomy and turn away from full reliance on their true King.

Our first parents were enticed by the promise of complete freedom from God to live as their own "gods," free to choose their own way, with boundless and unlimited opportunities previously unknown to them. They believed the lie, willingly rebelled, and ate from the tree — the very tree that God had warned them not to eat from. It was a dreadful decision with consequences that echo throughout eternity. Adam and Eve, and all those who would come after them, now became the objects of God's just anger and sobering judgment, suffering the punishment of death (physical and spiritual) and removal from Eden.

The sad reality of our fall into sin is a gospel truth that we need to remember whenever we deal with the motives and desires of our own hearts. The fall gives us perspective on our lives, reminding us of why we struggle and of the root cause behind all human suffering and frustration. As we shepherd others, we must remember to speak the truth of our sinful rebellion to one another. Martin Luther writes:

> To doubt the good will of God is an inborn suspicion of God with all of us. In all these difficulties we have only one support, the gospel of Christ. To hold on to it, that is the trick ... All these things cry out against us, death thunders at us, the devil roars at us. In the midst of the clamor the Spirit of Christ cries in our hearts, "Abba, Father" ... The Spirit cries because of our weakness ... [and] is sent forth into our hearts to assure us of the grace of God.[22]

Because you live in a fallen world, the truth is that all of your life you will struggle with doubting God.

The act of human rebellion created at least four primary separations. Human beings were separated from the *creation* (Genesis 3:17–19); we were separated in our relationships with *others* (Genesis 3:12, 16); we were separated from *God* and his loving presence and now have true moral guilt before us (Genesis 3:10, 22); and we were separated from *ourselves*. Our hearts and minds became darkened, our thinking futile (without reference to God), and we became spiritually dead, enslaved to sin. The apostle Paul summed it up this way: "Nothing good dwells in me ... I have the desire to do what is right, but not the ability to carry it out" (Romans 7:18–19).

The Bible tells us that because of our rebellion, we have strayed from our original purpose and turned away from a God-centered focus to a self-centered focus: "All we like sheep have gone astray; we have turned—every one—to his own way" (Isaiah 53:6). Self is now at the center of each of our lives. Each one of us is alienated from the creation, from one another, and, most importantly, from God. We have become enemies of God. Our labors must now be made "right" once again to be acceptable to God. We are more than just empty; we are broken, living under a curse of death that is eternal, spiritual, and physical. Our brokenness leads to a lifelong struggle as we try to find a way to be whole once again—a way back to the garden!

REDEMPTION: GOOD NEWS IN JESUS ALONE

Jesus Christ, God the Son, joyfully obeyed God the Father, who sent him to rescue his rebellious creation. Jesus was miraculously born of a virgin (he was sinless); God became a man. He willingly paid the price for our rebellion—spiritual, eternal, and physical death—by dying on a cross. Then he was raised back to life to demonstrate his complete victory over sin and death.

Jesus came to establish his kingdom rule and to redeem (buy back for himself at a price) a people of his own possession. The entire Old Testament—its laws, ceremonies, stories, characters, kings, prophets, and promises—is an uncompleted story of which Jesus is the fulfillment, the climax. Jesus is, as C. S. Lewis puts it, "the chapter on which the whole plot turns."[23] In Jesus, God kept the promise he had made: "The perfectly innocent died to rescue the hopelessly guilty. He took the place on a cross rightfully meant for us, to pay for sins we've committed and will commit against God."[24]

The gospel is the greatest proof of God's love for us. We deserved to be punished for our sins, but God put all of our sins on Jesus and punished him in our place. The Bible teaches that those who are saved by the death of Christ are also given the perfect righteousness of Jesus: "For our sake he [God the Father] made him [Jesus Christ] to be sin who knew no sin, so that in him we might become the righteousness of God" (2 Corinthians 5:21). It is a wonderful, beautiful exchange—our sin for his righteousness.

But the death of Christ was not the end of the story. Three days after his crucifixion, Jesus was raised back to life, and his resurrection gives us the certainty of eternal life. Forty days after his resurrection, Jesus returned to heaven, where he reigns today as the rightful King of his creation. Steve Childers, associate professor of practical theology at Reformed Theological Seminary, writes:

> The good news of the kingdom is that our king has won a marvelous victory for us. Through his sinless life, sacrificial death as our substitute, resurrection, and ascension, he has not only conquered death for us, removing its penalty, but he has also conquered sin's power over us ... Now, through repentance and faith, God means for us to tap into the powerful victory of our

king, so that we might be transformed into true worshipers of God and more authentic lovers of people ... Through faith we are always to be placing our affections on Christ.[25]

RESTORATION: A FUTURE WITH JESUS

The gospel is a declaration of how we are made right with God. But it is a message — a story — that changes everything. Christ has come to make all things new!

Robert Heppe, pastor at New Life Masih Ghar in London, England, wrote the following:

> The gospel is God's message of liberation: from guilt, alienation, and every bondage that hinders the human race from being fruitful for and reflecting the glory of God. The good news that Jesus preached is that he, as Lord of the cosmos, is now in the business of recapturing a runaway planet. He came to destroy the works of the Devil — all of them, not merely the psychological ones that plague middle-class people — and to bring the world under his saving authority. That means he came to reverse the effects of the fall, "as far as the curse is found." The gospel of the kingdom announces nothing less than God's intention and activity to replace the effects of the fall (sin, guilt, sickness, hunger, injustice, oppression, poverty, bondage, dehumanization, and death) with his kingdom righteousness; and his work will not be finished until his redemption covers the whole earth.[26]

As God's new people, we have become change agents in our world. We are "children of God without blemish ... [who] shine as lights in the world" (Philippians 2:15). We are witnesses of the risen Christ. The gospel is the power of God for saving *and* renewing us. God has given us a citizenship in heaven that allows us to serve him in the here and now. Coaching leaders with a clear grasp of the gospel and an understanding of God's desire and his plan to make all things new can have a shaping influence on their ministry in God's kingdom. Through Jesus and his work on our behalf we are now freed to serve with his power and love, not for ourselves in our own strength and wisdom. The gospel encourages humble dependence on God, along with creativity and courage that flow from authentic faith in the one who is risen, ruling, and returning one day to judge the living and the dead. The gospel gives a basis for coaching others, encouraging them to walk in the freedom and joy of God's good news.

One day there will be a new heaven and a new earth that will be completely free of sin and selfishness — a place of perfect friendship with God, others, and all of creation. God's original purpose will flourish, as those who have trusted in his rescue will enter into the grand purpose of worshiping him by loving him, serving him, and enjoying relationship with him forever.

One of the most amazing realities of this new world is that we will be with God forever, experiencing his complete and perfect joy. We will be restored to a perfect relationship with the one who created, loved, died, and was raised for us. C. S. Lewis, the well-known scholar and children's author, spoke of this first step into this new world as the real beginning to the story — "Chapter One of the Great Story which no one on earth has read: which goes on forever: in which every chapter is better than the one before."[27]

The gospel story is God's good news. Though I was alienated from God and under his just condemnation, living a life full of doubt and disobedience, God loved me and gave himself for me. Christ died on a cross, paying my debt with God, and rose alive from death to forgive my doubt and disobedience; to be my righteousness; to be my power to believe God, to say yes to him in worship and to say no to sin; to live a life of love for others; and to get me home with great joy. To live by the gospel is to rely on Jesus for all of our life and strength, to turn away from self-oriented beliefs and lifestyles. To the degree that the reality of the gospel story grips us, to that degree, we will begin to see life transformation occurring.

> Then I saw a new heaven and a new earth ... God himself will be with them as their God. He will wipe away every tear from their eyes, and death shall be no more, neither shall there be mourning nor crying nor pain anymore, for the former things have passed away.
> —Revelation 21:1, 3–4

As the affections of the heart (our inner motivations, drives, and desires) rest more and more on the beauty, wonder, and freedom of the gospel of grace—as it begins to take our breath away—the things of this world (and it, too, is filled with things that can take our breath away), things of our own flesh (our plans and personal strategies to be "right"), and the whispers of the evil one begin to lose their hold over us.

The gospel is more than just the power of God to save us; it is the power of God to sanctify us, to make us the very people the gospel declares us to be. In this sense, the gospel is just as necessary for Christians to hear (followers of Christ) as it is for unbelievers (those who do not know Christ). Dick Kauffmann of Harbor Presbyterian, a network of churches in San Diego, puts it this way:

> The gospel is God's explosive power that changes everything.
>
> First, the gospel makes us Christians ... God forgives your sin, declares you righteous in Christ, gives you eternal life, adopts you as his child, and ushers you into an intimate relationship with himself ...
>
> Second, the gospel grows us. The gospel is not merely the way we enter the kingdom; it is also the way we make all progress in kingdom living ... It is the way of righteousness "from first to last" ... Since the gospel not only makes us Christians (justification), but also grows us as Christians (sanctification), the most desperate need of both unbelievers and believers ... is to hear and appropriate the gospel to their lives.
>
> Third, the gospel empowers us to serve.... The gospel gives us a whole new motivational structure ... We will motivate with the gospel, which sets us free to love and serve unconditionally in response to God's grace in Christ.[28]

In other words, the gospel is the motive and the means for all that we do in life and in ministry. In the work of coaching, we find that when both coach and ministry leader are operating under the influence of the Holy Spirit, regularly applying the gospel story to each other's lives, praying together, encouraging one another, and allowing appropriate times of heart examination along with any necessary skill training, God is glorified, and the kingdom is advanced.

The gospel is the missing piece in the coaching process. Even with the best of intentions, the advice and wisdom of a seasoned coach will often begin with a perspective that assumes the solution to our problems lies within. But the gospel story starts in an entirely different place—with God, his work in this world, and, most importantly, his work in Jesus Christ. Coaching leaders with the gospel story is essential for an effective and life-changing coaching experience because the leader *needs* the gospel, those in their church *need* the gospel, the people the church is reaching in the community *need* the gospel, and our culture *needs* the gospel.

There is no greater need in the world today than for people to hear, understand, and respond to the message of the gospel. It starts with church leaders understanding it properly and communicating it clearly—in pulpits, in home groups, and in coaching relationships.

CHAPTER 3

THE PROBLEM WITH PERFORMANCE-CENTERED LEADERSHIP

I GREW UP IN A PERFORMANCE-CENTERED HOME. My parents were both hardworking people, and their entire approach to parenting and to life in general was a system of rewards, seeking the next goal, striving for great achievements. To be fair, my parents didn't know there was another way of parenting because that is how they had been reared. As of this writing, my dad is almost eighty-two years old, and he is still working hard. After forty-six years of employment in the same steel mill, he retired with a handsome pension, and for the past fifteen years he has worked at a golf course. I once asked him why he doesn't just quit and retire. In a gruff voice, he replied, "A man isn't worth anything if he doesn't work." That one phrase summarized in my mind his penchant for pursuing achievement. It also helped me understand where I had learned and acquired my own drive to achieve and succeed.

I want you to know that my parents are both very loving and supportive, and I continue to have a healthy relationship with them. But like many children, I was rewarded for accomplishing my daily checklist of home chores, doing well in my academic studies, and achieving athletic success. I remember being congratulated for hitting home runs, for leading the basketball team in scoring, for getting A's, and as a teenager in high school successfully running my own house painting business. Almost every affirmation I received from them was related to my performance. Unconsciously, I began to accept that I was valuable and worthy of love *only* when I performed exceptionally well.

And so I pushed myself in every area of my life. I knew I had to be the best. I would shoot baskets in my backyard until late into the night, dreaming of going to college on a scholarship (that was the only way I believed I'd be able to attend). I tried so hard in my pursuit of athletic excellence because I knew that my future rested on whether I could get recognized by the college scouts, get a scholarship, get a degree, and eventually run my own company. In my mind, every game I played felt like it was a matter of life or death. I fought hard to avoid failing. As a result, I turned the achievement of success in basketball into my god; it became my idol, and my entire life revolved around it. Eventually, I received my scholarship and was accepted into a small college. At the very first practice, as I was preparing to be one of the starting five on the team as a freshman, I broke my ankle. I remember heading back to my dorm room and punching a hole in the closet door. That hole was a continual reminder that my dreams were falling apart. Without basketball, I felt like I had lost my identity. So I turned to alcohol to numb the pain. But it didn't help.

On the last day of my first year of college, I was caught driving my truck on the college campus lawn. The police said they would release me from their custody if I left town immediately. I drove home late that night with my two best friends beside me in the front seat of my truck, and I fell asleep at the wheel. My vehicle veered off the road and hit the back of a van parked on the side of the highway, and in an instant my life was changed forever.

The damage to the front of the truck had jammed my door shut, so I climbed out of the window and found that I couldn't stand up on my legs. These were the legs that I had proudly used to run and jump and dunk, the legs that had afforded me an opportunity to attend college. Forced to my knees on the side of the road, I cried out to God, knowing that he was pursuing me, and I told him that I would stop running away from him. Freed from my self-reliance and strength, I humbly let him know that he could do whatever he wanted with me now. When I stood back up , I could no longer feel the pain in my legs. Quite literally, I have been walking with Jesus ever since that night.

A few years later, I felt God's call to enter vocational ministry as a youth pastor—but I soon learned that I hadn't quite left behind my performance-centered mentality. As a young pastor, I was "successful," and my work in this area simply fueled my desire for greater success. Others would applaud my efforts when I succeeded (the numbers would increase), and when numbers would drop, my boss would quickly chastise me. In response, I worked even longer hours, striving to excel, until I found I was consistently putting in seventy-five to ninety hours a week. Despite my extra effort, though, it was still not satisfactory for my boss. So I left that church, taking a call as a lead pastor at another church, hoping I would no longer need to work to please others and satisfy their desires.

Unfortunately, though I was now my own "boss," I dragged that same performance-centered ailment into this new church as well. My initial experiences of success drove me further into pursuing an elusive goal, and I worked countless hours at the expense of my marriage. I reasoned that my loving wife would understand. At first, I justified working long hours by telling myself it would increase the attendance of the church to the point where its offerings could sustain the church expenses. But after that was accomplished, I continued to work hard to satisfy my own ego and pride and to gain recognition. There were times when I would even think that my marriage was somehow getting in the way of accomplishing more for Jesus. Though it sounds bizarre to me now, my pride craved success, prestige, and recognition, and most of my relationships got in the way of trying to please the never-satisfied idol of approval, fueled by my performace.

A few years later, while I was praying alone backstage in preparation to preach to a large crowd of college students, the Holy Spirit spoke to my spirit, saying, "Shut up!" (That is the best way the Comforter gets my attention.) His word to me stopped me in my tracks. Then I sensed the Spirit saying to me, "Now preach to yourself." This wasn't an audible word, but it was real, and I knew it was for me. I didn't know how to respond, so I started reading over my notes. As I read, I saw them in a new way, as if I were preaching this message to myself, and I found that what I had written to share with others was exactly what the Spirit wanted to say to *me*. That experience of conviction began a process of self-discovery, learning that I had created an idol of success, worshiping my own achievements because I believed that these things gave me value and worth. I realized I wasn't really trusting God's provision of worth and value through his Son; I was trusting in my own ability to earn that value. I was more confident in my own strength than in God's omnipotent power. I began repenting of my blatant and foolish pride, just minutes before walking on the stage to teach.

PERFORMANCE-CENTERED LIVING

This experience gave me the insight to develop the following diagram, which helped me diagnose my tendency to live a performance-centered life (see Figure 4).

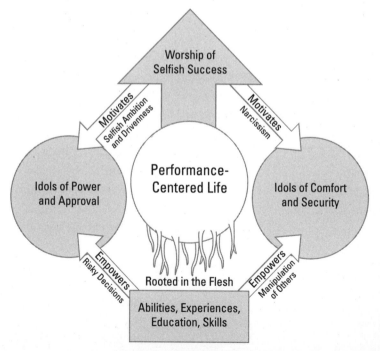

Figure 4: The Performance-Centered Life

LIVING BY THE FLESH

In the diagram, performance is at the center of this church leader's life and leadership. Performance is rooted in the flesh (Galatians 5:16–17). The leader is motivated by selfish success, and their drive to perform is rooted in the person's abilities, experiences, education, and skills. The desired outcomes are power, approval, comfort, and security. To gain power and approval, a leader characteristically will be driven to make risky decisions, decisions rooted in their own self-confidence. To achieve comfort and security, a leader will promote themselves and use others for their own benefit.

A performance-centered person functionally rejects the centrality of the gospel and slavishly responds to a craving to please their own flesh. Living by the flesh is how the Bible describes our tendency to follow our sin-desiring self instead of walking in step with the Spirit of God. When a person lives by their flesh, they believe that pleasing their own desires is more justifying—earning them worth, value, and favor with God—than living in line with the gospel. This person relies on their own way of salvation and ultimately rejects the gospel.

Our sinful desires are heart motivations that drive our behaviors. When these motivations begin to drive us, they become "over-desires," or what the Bible refers to as "lusts"—longings and deep desires of our hearts, sometimes for things forbidden and sometimes for making good things into ultimate things. Galatians 5 lists fifteen of these works of the flesh. By studying these fifteen sinful desires, we can identify five interrelated categories in this partial list of fleshly sins: sexual sins, relational sins, religious sins, materialistic sins, and indulgent sins.

Our desires are controlled by our needs, and at the most fundamental level these sinful desires are driven by four overriding needs common to every human heart. Heart idols are objects of our desire that control our choices and emotions by becoming our first love. Such idolatry is all-encompassing, and we can identify four idols that stand out as meta-categories: power, approval, comfort, and security.

Let's take a closer look and see how these four idols relate to the five categories of fleshly sins in Galatians 5:

Sexual sins include sins of sexual immorality, impurity, and sensuality. The *power idol* uses sex to control or hurt another person. The *approval idol* uses sex as a means to find approval from one's lover. The *comfort idol* uses sex as a way to feel better and to provide comfort for the soul's pains. The *security idol* uses sex as a way to find a false sense of security in one's relationship or control over the other person.

Relational sins include enmity, strife, jealousy, anger, rivalries, dissensions, and divisions. The *power idol* takes control of relationships through strength, intelligence, mind games, threats, and anger. The *approval idol* uses relationships to feel whole or right about one's self, especially if a person feels loved or respected by another person. The *comfort idol* uses relationships to feel whole if other people (parents, friends, and so forth) provide a happy relationship. The *security idol* uses relationships as a means to get things done and to feel productive.

Religious sins include idolatry and sorcery, the occult, living in a self-righteous way, and relying on legalism to seek satisfaction or wholeness. The *power idol* uses adherence to the rules or moral codes and disciplines of religion to earn personal righteousness. The *approval idol* uses religion to feel "right with oneself" by fitting in with others in the community. The *comfort idol* uses religion and its rules as a standard to measure their peace with themselves and their god. The *security idol* uses religion to determine if they're safe in the manner they are living their life.

Materialistic sins include envy, evil desires, and covetousness, which is idolatry (Colossians 3:5). Materialism finds wholeness to life in financial portfolios, nice homes, investment properties, new vehicles, clothing, technology, and in any other kind of material goods. The *power idol* uses a person's net worth to take advantage of people and situations. The *approval idol* uses materialism to display to others why they are acceptable. The *comfort idol* uses materialism to feel a sense of ease in and around their things. The *security idol* uses materialism to get the things they want and to provide the lifestyle they desire.

Indulgent sins include drunkenness, getting high, orgies, and things like these. The *power idol* has a sense of entitlement to indulge in lascivious lifestyles. The *approval idol* uses indulgence to be included among others, partying in sin. The *comfort idol* uses indulgence to ease pain and to experience an intoxicating feeling—even if it is temporary. The *security idol* uses indulgence to remove inhibitions among others and to take advantage of their lost sense of justice and goodness.

As you can see, the four source idols of the heart encompass most categories of sin. And for each of these idols and for our every sinful desire, the gospel is the only solution to our innate need for power, approval, comfort, and security. In the gospel we see the all-powerful, omnipotent Son of God using his power to serve us in our great need. And now his power is available to us as well, as we follow him in serving others.

We find that Jesus did not seek to earn approval but received it freely as a gift from his Father, and he has now given us the only approval we will ever need. The gospel tells us that we are completely accepted by the Father through the satisfactory work of Jesus. The Father provides us with the true comfort our hearts and lives need, and he has purchased our complete security, both now and into eternity, through the person and work of Jesus Christ. Only Jesus can offer us what our hearts really need, and only Jesus is worthy of our worship. Everything else is an idol that cannot satisfy.

The Scriptures tell us that God created "man and put him in the garden of Eden to work it and keep it" (Genesis 2:15). He made us in his image as creators, inventors, designers, and engineers in our culture. He also made us to "keep it," that is, to protect his creation, manage it, maintain it, and preserve it. As with anything else, we typically abuse the perfect plan that God intended for our lives. Because of this, we work too hard at the expense of other areas of responsibility for our own glory. We seek self-glory while sacrificing our relationships, our families, our values, our testimony, and our service for God. Additionally, we try to protect our personal domain at any cost. We can end up valuing our own comfort over community, turning our homes into our functional heaven and failing to extend hospitality, fearing that it will create discomfort in our lives.

God wants us to be fruitful, to multiply, and to prosper like a tree planted by streams of water (Psalm 1:3). We can interpret this to mean that there is nothing wrong with the acquisition of worldly success, fame, and fortune. But we cannot turn a good thing into an ultimate thing, or it immediately becomes a bad thing—a snare that captures the affections of our heart, replacing God on the throne of our lives. It becomes an idol, and that idol is usually hidden somewhere deep within our hearts.

As gospel coaches, we must learn to look for what the disciple-leader we coach is worshiping, what is driving their desires. How? By listening closely to their answers to our questions. This will not always be immediately obvious. It will involve exploring the implications of their inner motivations, discovering how they view success and what they are trying to accomplish in their lives. It will involve listening to the ways in which they seek power and comfort, where they find approval, and what helps them to feel like they are in control.

SELF AS OUR FUNCTIONAL SAVIOR

Selfish success, as an ultimate aim, is a lustful god that can never be satisfied. Success, in and of itself, is neutral. It is possible to be "successful" and yet avoid the snare of sacrificing everything at the altar of this idol. Yet it is still a common trait among many church leaders. We may desire success in various ways—in our finances, through our family, in our occupation or career, through our relationships, in the academic world, through maintaining good health, even in our sexuality. Success is a false indicator of God's love for us; neither does it tell us anything about God's lack of love for us. When we are successful, we can easily become prideful, thinking we are entitled to what we have achieved. In essence, we say, "I deserve this because I am successful." On the other hand, if we do not experience success, we may be inclined to feel a sense of guilt, shame, and despair. We find ourselves longing for success, no matter what it may cost. It can become a temptation, a snare to our hearts, much like the evil prostitute portrayed in the book of Proverbs. With her smooth words, she seduces a man into her bed and enslaves him in his own lust (Proverbs 5 and 6). Selfish success alluringly tempts us away from common sense and satisfaction in the person of Jesus Christ.

BUILDING SUCCESS ON OUR OWN ABILITIES

To be successful, we believe we must improve our competence, our experience, and our creativity. We say things like, "If it's gonna be, it's up to me," or, "If I believe it, I can achieve it." We wrongly put into practice the belief that our lives are built on our own strength and ability. We forget that as a revered Pharisee, the apostle Paul had every reason to boast in his own abilities, yet he saw them as worthless when he considered the value of what he had been freely given in Christ:

> Look out for the dogs, look out for the evildoers, look out for those who mutilate the flesh. For we are the circumcision, who worship by the Spirit of God and glory in Christ Jesus and *put no confidence in the flesh*—though I myself have reason for *confidence in the flesh* also. If anyone else thinks he has reason for *confidence in the flesh*, I have more: circumcised on the eighth day, of the people of Israel, of the tribe of Benjamin, a Hebrew of Hebrews; as to the law, a Pharisee; as to zeal, a persecutor of the church; as to righteousness under the law, *blameless*. But whatever gain I had, I counted as loss for the sake of Christ. Indeed, I count everything as loss because of the surpassing worth of knowing Christ Jesus my Lord. For his sake I have suffered the loss of all things and *count them as rubbish*, in order that I may gain Christ and be found in him, *not having a righteousness of my own* that comes from the law, *but that which comes through faith in Christ*, the righteousness from God that depends on faith—that I may know him and the power of his resurrection, and may share his sufferings, becoming like him in his death, that by any means possible I may attain the resurrection from the dead.
>
> —Philippians 3:2–11, emphasis mine

Paul warned against relying on success that was based on our own abilities. We are exhorted to put *no* confidence in the flesh regarding our salvation. Many people, even those called to leadership in the church, want to "partner" with God as a co-savior and are prone to think God needs our performance to accomplish his purpose for his church. In this passage, Paul highlights his own stellar life as a model Pharisee as an example of the futility of confidence in our own abilities. The nearly perfect life he lived was nothing but "rubbish." In using the Greek word *skybalon*, Paul declares his life to be nothing better than *dung*, the excrement of animals, something that was worthless and detestable.

Those who desire to become gospel coaches, guiding people in the diagnoses of their heart motivations and encouraging them with the truth of the gospel, should be aware of the prevalence of this performance-based motivation among many Christian leaders today. More than anything else, this is the means by which most people are appraised, valued, and promoted to positions of authority and honor—yes, even in the church.

Bob Osborne, executive director of World Harvest Mission, has observed that ministry leaders often drink a poisonous cocktail of narcissism and isolation. When leaders focus on their own success, the natural outcome is a self-consumed life. They are fighting, it seems, to be approved *and* to prove to others that they are successful. The outcome of a performance-centered life is a tendency to serve one of the four idols—power, approval, comfort, or security. To please any one of these and be considered a success, a person will inordinately drive themselves toward whatever the idol demands. A leader may seek to be applauded and gain a promotion at the expense of their health, family, and worship of God. Sadly, a limited measure of success will typically drive a person even more deeply into their idolatry in an effort to maintain their position of power, approval, comfort, and security. To maintain what they have gained, a leader may make some risky decisions, covering them under the banner of extreme faith. Likewise, a person who is seeking security may exercise whatever influence they have on other people to build an organization or amass financial resources or achieve some level of prominence whereby they feel in control of their life and these resources. They may manipulate people and circumstances to feed this idol of security.

THE ALTERNATIVE: GOSPEL-CENTERED LIVING

In a gospel-centered life (see Figure 5), we are indwelt and filled by the Holy Spirit to worship God. Rather than worshiping self (as in a

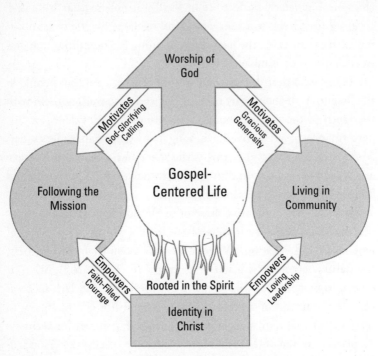

Figure 5: The Gospel-Centered Life

performance-centered model), we worship the one true God. We love the Lord with all our heart, with all our soul, with all our strength, and with our entire mind (Luke 10:27). Through the Spirit's empowerment, we set the Lord always before us; he is at our right hand, and we will not be shaken. Therefore our hearts are glad, and our whole being rejoices. Our flesh also dwells secure (Psalm 16:8–9).

Rather than resting in our own abilities (as in the performance-centered life), a gospel-centered believer rests in their identity in Christ. In his epistles, the apostle Paul often used the expression "in Christ." To be "in Christ" means sharing in Christ's death and resurrection, being placed under his headship rather than under the curse of Adam. It means that we now live in a completely different relationship to God. Christ's death and resurrection are the foundations of this new, gospel-centered life. Dying with Christ means finding no life in the things that used to run our lives; it means living under a new rule and serving a new King. While self and success are the central motivations in a performance-centered life (expressed in varied ways), Christ calls us to do everything *for his glory* and not for our own. Being raised with Christ means rising to a new way of living under his kingship. Before we come under Christ's kingship, our identity is dominated by our own concerns rather than by loving God and loving people as Jesus did. Again, the apostle Paul is helpful in describing this new way of life, being "in Christ"—a new creation:

> Therefore, if anyone is in Christ, he is a new creation. The old has passed away; behold, the new has come. All this is from God, who through Christ reconciled us to himself and gave us the ministry of reconciliation; that is, in Christ God was reconciling the world to himself, not counting their trespasses against them, and entrusting to us the message of reconciliation.
>
> —2 Corinthians 5:17–19

POSITION IN CHRIST

Coaches can call disciple-leaders to repentance and simultaneously call them to live in accordance with their position in Christ. For example, this means that we reinforce that Christ has declared that we are heirs of God and fellow heirs with him (Romans 8:17), even though we may not be living as an heir of God would. In practice, we may be living as spiritual orphans, but positionally we *are* children of God. When my sons were younger, I would occasionally correct their behavior by reminding them of the gospel—that they are declared dead to sin and alive to Christ. Although they still had the desire to sin, they didn't have to obey that impulse any longer because they were positionally dead to sin and alive to Christ. I keep a list of these positional promises on my desk to remind me who I am declared to be in the Word of God. Even though I do not always *feel* this way, these Scriptures remind me of *who I am in Christ.*

Through Christ, I am dead to sin (Romans 6:11).
Through Christ, I am spiritually alive (Romans 6:11;
    1 Corinthians 15:22).

Through Christ, I am forgiven (Colossians 2:13; 1 John 2:12).

Through Christ, I am declared righteous (1 Corinthians 1:30; 2 Corinthians 5:21).

Through Christ, I am a child of God (Romans 8:16; Philippians 2:15).

Through Christ, I am God's possession (Titus 2:14).

Through Christ, I am an heir of God (Romans 8:17).

Through Christ, I am blessed with all spiritual blessing (Ephesians 1:3).

Through Christ, I am a citizen of heaven (Philippians 3:20).

Through Christ, I am free from the law (Romans 8:2).

Through Christ, I am crucified with him (Galatians 2:20).

Through Christ, I am free from the desires of the flesh (Galatians 5:24).

Through Christ, I am declared blameless and innocent (Philippians 2:15).

Through Christ, I am a light in the world (Matthew 5:14–15; Philippians 2:15).

Through Christ, I am victorious over Satan (Luke 10:19).

Through Christ, I am cleansed from sin (1 John 1:7).

Through Christ, I am set free in Christ from the power of sin (Colossians 2:11–15).

Through Christ, I am secure in him (1 Peter 1:3–5).

Through Christ, I am at peace with God (Romans 5:1; Philippians 4:6–9).

Through Christ, I am loved by God (1 John 4:10).

Our actions are determined by our identity. Who we are and how we see ourselves affect the choices we make and how we respond to circumstances. Knowing our identity is crucial. When Jesus was baptized, God the Father identified with Jesus by announcing, "This is my beloved Son, with whom I am well pleased" (Matthew 3:17). Immediately after this definitive declaration of Jesus' identity as the beloved Son, the pleasure of the Father, we learn that the Spirit led Jesus into the wilderness to be tempted by Satan for forty days. Why?

Then Jesus was led up by the Spirit into the wilderness to be tempted by the devil. And after fasting forty days and forty nights, he was hungry. And the tempter came and said to him, "If you are the Son of God, command these stones to become loaves of bread." But he answered, "It is written,

"'Man shall not live by bread alone,
    but by every word that comes from the mouth of God.'"

Then the devil took him to the holy city and set him on the pinnacle of the temple and said to him, "If you are the Son of God, throw yourself down, for it is written,

"'He will command his angels concerning you,'

and

"'On their hands they will bear you up,
    lest you strike your foot against a stone.'"

Jesus said to him, "Again it is written, 'You shall not put the Lord your God to the test.'" Again, the devil took him to a very high mountain and showed him all the kingdoms of the world and their glory. And he said to him, "All these I will give you, if you will fall down and worship me." Then Jesus said to him, "Be gone, Satan! For it is written,

"'You shall worship the Lord your God
    and him only shall you serve.'"

Then the devil left him, and behold, angels came and were ministering to him.

—Matthew 4:1–11

In the first two temptations, the Devil attacks Jesus' identity directly, questioning what the Father has just declared to be true: "*If you are the Son of God ...*" The Deceiver tempts Jesus with bread to satisfy his hunger and provide comfort, as well as with angelic rescue from a leap of death to prove his faith in God's approval and protection. Finally, the Devil offers him the power to rule over kingdoms of the world if Jesus will simply bow down and worship him. Hebrews 4 reminds us that Jesus was tempted in all ways, just as we are, and yet he never sinned. We see in this passage that Jesus was tempted with the idol of *power* (over the kingdoms), the idol of *approval* (if you are the Son of God), the idol of *comfort* (to eat stones-turned-into-bread after a forty-day fast), and the idol of *security* (by having angels rescue him). In response, Jesus rebukes Satan and quotes the Scriptures: "You shall worship the Lord your God and him only shall you serve."

We worship that which gives us our identity. As a church leader, you may be tempted to find your identity in your role as a pastor, a director of ministry, or a leader of a small group. Whatever you identify with, you worship. This is why our identity must rest in Christ.

TURNING THE CHURCH RIGHT SIDE UP

It is only from our identity in Christ that we are free to worship in spirit and in truth. People often walk into our worship gatherings with their hearts and minds completely alienated from God. When the worship leader asks them to stand and worship, they are thinking about how inadequate they are to worship God. They may view themselves as adulterers, addicts, lustful people, haters of others, alcoholics, losers, those unloved and unapproved. Or they may see themselves as righteous and moral because of all the good things they have done. Only when we view ourselves "in Christ" can we rightly worship. Our identity, informed and affected by the gospel, is the key to our worship.

The gospel is distorted when our attention is focused exclusively on the mission of God and the community of God's people. Church leaders are tempted to value things like greater mission expansion and a deeper experience of community, and they are often promoted or given positions of influence when they are successful at creating these things. This is a *horizontal* focus that will assuredly disappoint the church leader. Instead, mission and community should flow out of the *vertical* focus of *worship* and *identity*. It is helpful to remember that Jesus spent thirty years of his life preparing for just three years of ministry. He spent forty days alone with his Father and the Spirit in the wilderness prior to his public ministry. Even in the midst of his ministry, he intentionally spent extended times alone with God in prayer and fasting, separated from the mission and his community of disciples. His focus was vertical, rooted in his identity as the Son of God. He submitted to the will of God and cried out often to him in prayer. He taught that worship and prayer are connected (Luke 11:2).

Was this only true of Jesus? No, for we find a similar pattern in the life of the apostle Paul. Paul considered himself a "slave" of Jesus, submitted to the will of another. He spent three years alone in the Arabian wilderness learning from the risen Lord, and it would be another fourteen years before his first missionary journey. Glorifying God through worship that flows through the gospel, is empowered by the Spirit, and is rooted in our identity in Christ is the ultimate end of all things. This vertical, God-glorifying focus is how we turn the church right side up—not by making the mission of the church our primary goal. Effective mission and rich community flow out of worship and identity.

PASSION AND CALLING FOR THE MISSION OF JESUS

The fourfold outcome of a gospel-centered life is (1) the worship of God, (2) resting in our identity in Christ, (3) living in true community with God's people, and (4) following the mission of God. If we are worshiping God and following his Son, Jesus Christ, as Spirit-filled disciples, we will be fishing for men (Matthew 4:19). We will be making disciples of all nations, baptizing them in the name of the Father and of the Son and of the Holy Spirit, and teaching them to observe all that Jesus has commanded us (Matthew 28:19–20).

Rather than being driven by a selfish desire to be successful for our own glory, we're moved by a passion and calling from God on our lives to be image bearers and missionaries in obedience to Christ and for the glory of God. There's a subtle but distinct difference between God-inspired passion and a selfish drive. One is oriented around self-recognition, and the other around God's gaining a great reputation for himself. An effective gospel coach will help diagnose the difference between selfish ambition and God-honoring ambition.

A COMMUNITY OF GRACE AND LOVE

Flowing out of a worshipful life that is looking to Jesus, "the founder and perfecter of our faith" (Hebrews 12:1), is a heart of generosity. This generosity is motivated by a deep awareness that we ourselves have received grace. As a result, we extend that same grace to others as image bearers of Jesus. The apostle John writes:

> And the Word became flesh and dwelt among us, and we have seen his glory, glory as of the only Son from the Father, full of grace and truth ... And from his fullness we have all received, grace upon grace ... grace and truth came through Jesus Christ.
> —John 1:14, 16–17

The fruit of God's grace extended to others is a community of generosity. One clear sign of a gospel-empowered life is that one's generosity is motivated by the grace of God as opposed to a drive for power, approval, comfort, or security. It is easy for leaders in the church to seek positions of influence in an effort to gain a sense of security, power, comfort, or approval for themselves, but this only produces a narcissistic leader. A gospel coach must exercise wisdom and discernment to determine the difference between doing good works for selfish reasons and extending generosity to display the gospel of grace. One of the keys is noticing how important it is that others are aware of these acts of generosity. A narcissist does not typically demonstrate generosity unless someone is able to recognize it publicly.

COURAGE IN CHRIST LEADING TO MISSION

Because of our identity in Christ, we also exercise courage motivated by faith, that is, faith in Christ and not in ourselves: "I can do all things through [Christ] who strengthens me" (Philippians 4:13). Our righteousness is in Christ; our redemption is in Christ; our sanctification is in Christ; our wisdom is in Christ; our fruit bearing is in Christ; our power is in Christ; our joy is in Christ; our satisfaction is in Christ; our obedience is in Christ; our suffering is in Christ; our faith is in Christ; our rest is in Christ; our trust is in Christ; and our strength is in Christ.[1]

THE PERFORMANCE-CENTERED LIFE		THE GOSPEL-CENTERED LIFE	
Worship of Self	Flesh-Empowered Behavior	Worship of God	Spirit-Empowered Behavior
Power	Risky decisions	Mission	Faith-filled courage
Approval	Selfish ambitions and drivenness		Called to make disciples
Comfort	Narcissistic	Community	Gracious generosity
Security	Manipulation of others		Loving leadership

Table 1: Comparison of Two Leadership Styles

In Christ we display courage rooted in faith as we engage in the mission of God. A performance-centered life, however, will exhibit something more akin to risk taking, but it is really nothing more than accomplishing our own mission for our own glory, approval, or comfort. The difference between the two is once again subtle and hard to distinguish. Yet each can be recognized by their fruit over time. One brings glory to God, and the other brings glory to something or someone else — perhaps an organization or a person.

Through the identity we have in Christ, we are also able to effectively lead a community with love that is characteristic of a true shepherd. Our leadership is not simply a demonstration of our affection for others. Ultimately, it is a demonstration of Jesus' affection for us. We are not interested in manipulating or coercing others to do what we expect or desire them to do. Rather, we are occupied with shepherding others toward a common life together that exhibits the gospel through obedience to Christ.

Table 1 above shows the subtle difference between a gospel-centered life and a performance-centered life. The table on the left shows the behavior of the flesh-empowered life, while the table on the right shows that of the Spirit-empowered life. You can recognize the subtlety of the differences between life in the Spirit and life in the flesh. This highlights the fact that most of our motivations are not simply blatant attempts to sin. Rather, we most commonly feed our proclivity to sin *when we disregard the gospel empowerments of grace, love, faith, and calling.* As John Calvin once wrote, "Man's nature ... is a perpetual factory of idols," and, "Every one of us is, even from his mother's womb, expert in inventing idols."[2] The problem we face is that we are often quite ignorant of the idols in our lives.[3] They masquerade as subtle distortions of good, God-honoring desires.

JESUS' COMPARISON OF THE TWO LIFESTYLES

In Luke 18, Jesus compares a person who is performance centered with a person who is gospel centered. In verse 10, Jesus introduces us to two men who go up to the temple to pray—one a Pharisee, the other a tax collector.

Pharisees were members of the Jewish religious party and prominent religious leaders in Palestine during the time of Jesus, held in high regard by the people. They insisted that their unwritten oral traditions and interpretations of the law were binding on all Jews. But the Pharisees were also a prime example of religious people who were driven and who evaluated themselves and other people by their outward performance.

Tax collectors during the time of Jesus, on the other hand, were usually fellow Jews who worked for Rome, the foreign rulers. Also known as "publicans," they were generally described as greedy, often taking more money than they were entitled to. When they collected their taxes for Rome, they would turn over the required amount of money and keep whatever they could add on for themselves. They were known to extort large sums of money from the common people. So it's no surprise that Jesus chooses a tax collector in his story to illustrate the worst of sinners.

Jesus describes the religious, self-righteous Pharisee in the parable as a man preoccupied with his outward acts and moral superiority who prays, "God, I thank you that I am not like other men, extortioners, unjust, adulterers, or even like this tax collector. I fast twice a week; I give tithes of all that I get" (Luke 18:11–12). Jesus uses the Pharisee to illustrate a person trying to convince God and others of how righteous he is and how worthy he is of God's favor. This approach is typical of a performance-centered person who believes that their success is based on their own righteousness and ability, and that they are entitled to the fruits of their labor, even if it comes at the expense of others. Haven't we all prayed this way at one time or another in our life? "God, I'm serving you faithfully and tithing my money, so why did this terrible thing happen to me?" When we pray like this, we reveal an attitude in our hearts that we feel entitled to something from God because of our behavior and our obedience.

Jesus contrasts the Pharisee with the infamous tax collector. The tax collector stands far off from others and will not even lift his eyes to heaven, instead beating his breast, saying, "God, be merciful to me, a sinner!" (Luke 18:13). This awful sinner — a fact no one would question — does not rely on his own ability or righteousness or sense of entitlement but rather on the mercy of God as his only hope.

The conclusion of the story captures the essence of Jesus' teaching. We are told that the tax collector departs from the temple to his house *justified* — declared righteous by God — rather than the near-perfect Pharisee who had declared himself better than others based on his performance. Jesus concludes the parable with this teaching: "For everyone who exalts himself will be humbled, but the one who humbles himself will be exalted." Jesus is contrasting a performance-centered life that highlights one's abilities and achievements with a gospel-centered life lived in humble awareness of one's need for mercy. He pronounces judgment on the performance-centered life.

WHAT'S THE DIFFERENCE?

This doesn't mean that a gospel-centered person lacks productivity, neglects good deeds, or rejects success. In fact, a person who is gospel centered will likely accomplish much fruit for the kingdom and for the mission of God. But their success is not rooted in their performance or motivated by a desire for personal glory. This is the key difference—and it's a big difference! Gospel-centered productivity is not achieved through using others, manipulating them, or leading them by force. Neither is it driven by a need to produce results to promote one's own security or comfort. Rather, the efforts are rooted in the gospel and motivated by love for God and a humble willingness to serve others, to seek their good, and to put their needs before our own. And all of this is done to honor and bring glory to Christ, who was sent by the Father and now sends his church to continue his work through his body, the church—a gathered community of Spirit-filled disciples.

CHAPTER 4

THE ONLY SOLUTION TO THE STRESS OF CHURCH MINISTRY

AS GOSPEL COACHES, we are concerned about skill development and problem solving, but we are also committed to helping a person identify the underlying idols — the roots of their sin — and then coaching them in an appropriate response to that sin through ruthless confession and aggressive yet joyful repentance. Our goal is that they would walk in the freedom that Christ has purchased for them.

This spiritual coaching is done with a humble realization of our own sinful condition. We must begin by recognizing that we cannot do this alone. The bent of our own hearts as coaches is toward self; our natural tendency is to take our life into our own hands and to try to make it work apart from Christ. And there will be times when we doubt whether or not lasting change is possible. Even mature believers will struggle with doubts about God's love, goodness, and power at times. Martin Luther, one of the primary leaders of the Protestant Reformation, wrote this in his commentary on Galatians:

I myself have been preaching and cultivating [the gospel of grace] through reading and writing for almost twenty years and still feel the old clinging dirt of wanting to deal so with God that I may contribute something so that he will give me his grace in exchange for my holiness.

Part of coaching is remembering that the gospel isn't based on our goodness; it's based on the goodness of Jesus. Faith in Jesus Christ alone is our only way to be "right" with God and to be made whole. We must remember the truth that we receive both his *legal* righteousness and his *imputed* righteousness. We are forgiven of our rebellion and our disobedience to the law, and we are given all of Jesus' righteousness: "For our sake he [God] made him [Jesus] to be sin who knew no sin, so that in him [Jesus] we might become the righteousness of God" (2 Corinthians 5:21). Not only are we declared not guilty; we are also made fully righteous in Christ, and his righteous life of obedience is ours. This is what frees us from the condemnation of the law and from sin's ongoing power over us.

We must also learn to embrace the truth that we have been adopted into God's family as his sons and daughters. God has not only given us his friendship but has also taken us into his family as heirs of all that belongs to Christ. As J. I. Packer noted, "To be right with God the Judge is a great thing, but to be loved and cared for by God the Father is a greater thing."[1]

Jesus promised that he would send us the Holy Spirit. When you received Christ as Savior, you received the Holy Spirit and his power in your life. The gospel tells us that we can now say yes to the Spirit and obey God's commands to put on love, to forgive, to serve with our gifts and talents, and to practice mercy and justice. The gospel also empowers us to say no to the flesh. Paul writes, "For the grace of God has appeared, bringing salvation for all people, training us [literally, instructing us] to renounce [literally, to deny] ungodliness and worldly passions, and to live self-controlled, upright, and godly lives in the present age" (Titus 2:11–12).

Steve Brown, president of Key Life, writes these words:

When I became a Christian, two things happened. I got saved, and I got loved. I got loved so deeply that it still amazes me when I think about it. Because I got loved so deeply, I want to please the One who loved me that much. I may not always please him — sometimes I even run in the other direction, because his love can really hurt. I may chafe against pleasing him; I may not even speak to him. But I'll tell you something: I want to please him, and when I don't please him, it hurts. Now if I really want to please him, I must know what pleases him. I find that out by reading the Word and listening to his commandments. When I know what he wants, I want what he wants. Love does that to you. But I must know what he wants. That is why we must never soften the teaching of the law of God. Holiness is a very important teaching as long as it is given in the context of God's love.[2]

HEART IDOLS

The idols of our modern world are not necessarily the hand-carved statues of the ancient world. In their autonomous self-seeking ways, people have instead come to serve or worship the self-erected idols of power, approval, comfort, and security. We must ruthlessly inspect the sin in our heart for these idols. Since we are created to worship, we will inevitably center our lives on something to worship, whether we realize it or not. Worship is like a fire hose that has gotten stuck in the "on" position and is endlessly shooting water out with great force. We must decide where to aim the hose. That's choosing the focus of our worship.

In coaching others, it is vital that the coach get to the heart so as to identify the objects that have replaced or are hampering our worship of God. As Tim Keller puts it, "The solution to our sin problem is not simply to change our behavior, but to reorient and center our entire heart and life on God."[3] Therefore, we must go after sin by penetrating to the root and simply focusing on the fruit of the sin. There are times when people will repent of sin that is simply the fruit of the idol in their heart. This does not deal with the root cause of the sin; to do that, we must first learn the *why* of their behavior, not just the *what*.

In the next illustration (Figure 6), we see an example of a disciple who has been told that he is angry. His initial reaction to this problem will likely be to do better, to avoid conflict, to live at peace with others, and to establish barriers to shield him from being angry. The person may say that he is sorry for his anger and even promise never to do it again. But ultimately this approach—even though it deals with issues of sin and repentance—is rooted in Moralistic Therapeutic Deism. The problem with this all-too common response is that it fails to address the *motives of the heart* that lie beneath the sin of anger.

To change his behavior, this person must first understand the why of his behavior. He must learn to identify the false belief he has accepted and repent of the sin beneath his anger by uncovering the idol (his "functional savior" or what he believed would provide him with the power, approval, comfort, or security he desired). In this case, after several probing questions, the root issue underlying his anger is seen to be an idol of pride. By repenting of his pride and selfishness, the man is able to address the fruit of his idolatry, his sinful anger.

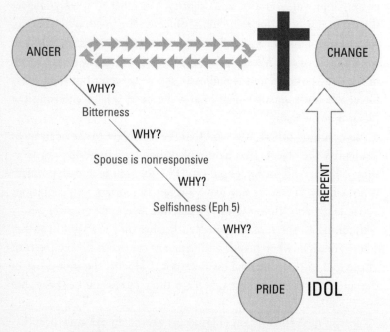

Figure 6: Exploring the Why beneath the What

Why is it so important to address the root idolatry of our sin? Unless we address the root of the problem—the heart idolatry—there will be no lasting change. To illustrate, consider the Deepwater Horizon drilling rig operated by BP. For almost three months in 2010, a seafloor oil gusher from the rig spilled 4.9 million barrels of crude oil into the Gulf Coast at the rate of 35,000 to 60,000 barrels per day. Approximately 623 miles of Gulf Coast shoreline were affected by the oil. Miles of strands of caramel-colored goo and globs of oil appeared on the beaches, and cleanup teams were sent to shovel off the beach. Addressing the apparent sins, such as anger, without addressing the sins beneath the sins is like merely removing the globs of oil from the beaches of the Gulf of Mexico and declaring the problem solved. What if BP had not capped the wellhead and merely kept removing the globs of oil? What if they only focused on the beaches? What if we only focus on our outward sins? We have to address the *source* of our sin for effective change to occur. We have to explore the *why* beneath the what to identify our root idols, repent of them, and replace our affection for them with a love for Christ.

MAKING GOOD THINGS INTO ULTIMATE THINGS

Our idols take various forms—power and success; approval; comfort and pleasure; control; security. Since true change only occurs when we repent of and turn from the deep-seated idols in our lives, a key aspect of gospel coaching is learning to identify our idols and repent of them. Just as we can't kill a tree by cutting off a few branches, we also can't hope to defeat sin by simply feeling bad about its outcomes. Mark Driscoll, pastor of Mars Hill Church, Seattle, Washington, unpacked the idea of idolatry in a sermon titled "Resisting Idolatry Like Jesus," based on 1 Corinthians 10:1–14:

> The tricky thing about idolatry is that it is usually the pursuit of something that is otherwise good … Idolatry is enslavement to something we love … it's a good thing that is elevated to a god thing. [So how can we figure out what our idols are?] … Define for yourself your "little hell." For you, hell is being poor; for you, it's being ugly; for you, it's being fat; for you, it's being unloved; for you, it's being underappreciated. The fear of your hell compels

you to choose for yourself a false savior god to save you from that hell … For those whose hell is being unmarried, your savior will be a spouse. For those whose hell is loneliness, you will choose for yourself a friend or group of friends or a pet—you will do anything for them because they are your functioning saviors from your hell of loneliness.[4]

Let's look again at the idols of power, approval, comfort, and security listed in the table below (Table 2) and discover how we create idols in our hearts. How do we end up making good things into ultimate things? A sin becomes an idol when we value it more than we value Jesus as our ultimate joy and satisfaction. In doing this, we reject God as our object of worship and replace him with something else.

Since our idols are the things we treasure and value more than Jesus, we discover them by honestly asking what gives our life meaning, worth, and value. Consider the following table. Which of these idols give your life meaning? What are the things you treasure, that give your life value and worth?

Our new "saviors" make promises to provide us with meaning or worth—ways in which we will achieve wholeness. But these self-made idols also threaten us, warning us that if we do not serve them, our lives will be worthless, meaningless, and empty. We start out

Power Idol	Approval Idol
• control • position • influence • success • strength (exerted)	• relationships • achievement • ethnicity • social circles • appearance
Security Idol	**Comfort Idol**
• family • finances • protection • religion • safety • future	• pleasure • health • freedom • excesses • home and vehicles • recreation

Table 2: Table of Idols

by asking them to serve us, but eventually their allure is too strong. They overtake us, mastering our desires and ending up controlling almost every aspect of our lives.

True, lasting change can only occur when we *repent* of the deep-seated idols we have trusted in and in *faith* believe in the gospel of Jesus Christ, relying on him as our only means of salvation. Gospel coaching moves beyond the outward, methodologically driven process that often characterizes coaching to the motivational, heart level of the disciple-leader. Gospel coaches direct a person in a process of repentance and faith, releasing their idolatry to trust in Christ.

Martin Luther set off the Protestant Reformation by nailing the ninety-five theses to the door of Castle Church in Wittenberg, Germany. The very first of these theses emphasizes the essential importance of repentance in the Christian life: "Our Lord and Master Jesus Christ ... willed that the whole life of believers should be repentance."[5] Richard Lovelace reminds us of this as well, pointing out that all repentance involves confronting unbelief with faith in the truth of the gospel:

> Luther was right: the root behind all other manifestations of sin is compulsive unbelief — our voluntary darkness concerning God, ourselves, his relationship to the fallen world, and his redemption purpose ... If the fall occurred through the embracing of lies, the recovery process of salvation must center on faith in truth, reversing this condition."[6]

The gospel's two dynamics of repentance and faith, leading to obedience, are the only solution to the ongoing battle of unbelief. Obedience flows from the freedom of the gospel.

It is necessary for a gospel coach to know what repentance truly looks like if they are to help their disciple develop a life of continual repentance. Thomas Watson, English Puritan (c. 1620 – 1686), wrote a helpful treatise on repentance. He stated, "Repentance is a grace of God's Spirit whereby a sinner is inwardly humbled and visibly reformed."[7] John the Baptist warned the Pharisees and Sadducees who were arriving with bath towels at his baptism, "You brood of vipers! Who warned you to flee from the wrath to come? Bear fruit in keeping with repentance" (Matthew 3:7-8). Both John the Baptist and Thomas Watson tell us that a change of life — visible fruit — accompanies repentance.

Watson identified six ingredients necessary for true repentance.[8] The first is *sight of sin*, whereby a person comes to themselves (Luke 15:17) and clearly views their lifestyle as sinful. If a disciple fails to see their sin, they are rarely motivated to repent. Many times a person needs help from their gospel coach to recognize the severity and extent of their wrongness.

The second ingredient for true repentance is *sorrow for sin* (Psalm 38:18). We need to feel the nails of the cross in our soul as we sin. Repentance includes godly grief, a holy agony (2 Corinthians 7:10). A gospel coach is careful not to let the disciple out of the grieving posture before true, sorrowful repentance is experienced. Coaches must allow those they disciple some time to delve into the darkness of their sin to fully drive it out before bringing comfort (Psalm 126:5). The fruits of repentance will be expressed in genuine, anguishing sorrow over the offense itself and not just its consequences. This sorrow for sin is more than just a "worldly grief"; it will be seen in the ongoing actions it produces. True repentance lingers in the soul and not just on the lips. The sorrowful repenter prays, "Lord, I know what I did was evil. My heart elevated something besides you to an idol, making it my god."

The third ingredient is *confession of sin*. The humble sinner voluntarily passes judgment on themselves as they sincerely admit to the specific sins of their heart. We must not relent of our confession until all of it is freely and fully admitted. We must pluck up any hidden root of sin within us. "Beware lest there be among you a root bearing poisonous and bitter fruit" (Deuteronomy 29:18). In the Scriptures, we find at least seven benefits to confession:

1. Confession of sin gives glory to God. (Joshua 7:19)
2. Confession of sin is a means to humble the soul. (2 Chronicles 26:19)
3. Confession of sin gives release to a troubled heart. (Psalm 51:11-12)
4. Confession of sin purges out sin. (Nehemiah 3:13) Augustine called it "the expeller of vice."
5. Confession of sin endears Christ to the soul that needs atoning. (Romans 7:25)

6. Confession of sin makes way for forgiveness.
   (2 Samuel 12:13; 1 John 1:9)
7. Confession of sin makes way for mercy. (Proverbs 28:13)

Here one may pray, "Lord, I am sorry for making something other than you my savior, and I no longer choose to live under its control. I repent of rejecting your cross and making my own way."

Fourth, *shame for sin* is an ingredient for true repentance. The color of repentance is blushing red. Repentance causes a holy bashfulness. Ezra prayed, "O my God, I am ashamed and blush to lift my face to you, my God, for our iniquities have risen higher than our heads, and our guilt has mounted up to the heavens" (Ezra 9:6). The repenting prodigal was so ashamed of his sin that he did not feel he deserved to be a son anymore (Luke 15:21). Sin makes us shamefully naked and deformed in God's eyes and puts Christ to shame, the one who took the scorn of the cross on himself.

The fifth ingredient in repentance is *hatred of sin*. We must hate our sin to the core. We hate sin more deeply when we love Jesus more fully. Repentance begins with the love of God and ends with hatred of sin. As gospel coaches, we must help disciple-leaders identify every sin that sprouts in the garden of their heart and is fueled by the fertilizer of apathy toward Christ. Tolerating sin is a willful leap toward committing it. True repentance loathes sin deeply.

Finally, the sixth progressive ingredient of repentance is *turning from sin and returning to the Lord* "with all your heart" (Joel 2:12). This turning from sin implies a notable change, "performing deeds in keeping with their repentance" (Acts 26:20). Ezekiel records these words of God to the house of Israel: "Repent and turn away from your idols, and turn away your faces from all your abominations" (Ezekiel 14:6). We are called to turn away from *all* our abominations—not just the obvious ones or the ones that create friction in others. The goal of repentance is not to manufacture peace among others with perfunctory repentance, but rather to turn to God wholly.

Most importantly, though, this repentance is not just a turning away from sin; it is also a turning "of repentance toward God and of faith in our Lord Jesus Christ" (Acts 20:21). A gospel coach should invite the disciple-leader to joyfully repent of his doubt by believing in the gloriousness, goodness, greatness, and graciousness of God and to turn in faith to trust in the freedom Christ offers in the gospel. Repentance is rooted in a hatred of sin *and* a joyful awareness of God's loving-kindness, which leads to joy: "God's kindness is meant to lead you to repentance" (Romans 2:4). We rejoice that Christ has done everything for us—all that we need to secure our salvation and our growth in holiness. Our prayer is, "Lord, I am an adopted child, not a slave to sin. I am accepted because of Christ. I have forgotten how loved, secure, rich, and free I am in Christ. Please let me be astonished by your love."

GOSPEL TRANSFORMATION: YOU CAN CHANGE

While idol identification and rejection are necessary in repentance, true and lasting change is not complete without turning in faith toward God. My friend Tim Chester writes about this transformative process: "Sinful acts always have their origin in some form of unbelief. Behind every sin is a lie."[9] He identifies megatruths about

Power Idol	Approval Idol
God is *glorious*, so I don't have to produce results.	God is *gracious*, so I don't have to prove myself.
• has to be in a position of power • is demanding • wants final decision • thwarts other leaders • has bursts of anger	• takes criticism and failure badly • finds it hard to relax • is proud or envious of others • desires inclusion • craves recognition
Security Idol	**Comfort Idol**
God is *great*, so I don't have to be in control.	God is *good*, so I don't have to look elsewhere for comfort, peace, and fulfillment.
• is overbearing • is inflexible • is impatient • is irresponsible • hides weaknesses	• feels ministry is a burden • often complains • makes people feel a burden of duty • lacks joy • has inconsistent moods

Table 3: A Diagnosis of Unbelief

God that when we forget, lead to turning away from him. In the final move of repentance, we reaffirm the truth to our hearts that God is glorious (negating the idol of power); God is gracious (negating the idol of approval); God is good (addressing the idol of comfort); and God is great (countering the idol of security).[10]

Scotty Smith, founding pastor of Christ Community Church in Franklin, Tennessee, writes the following:

> The truth and beauty of the gospel expose these idol-myths as feeble substitutes and garish counterfeits. And the power of the gospel enables us to break free from their enslaving and destructive grasp. Indeed, as our deliverer and liberator, Jesus is freeing us for the great adventure of living as *characters in* and *carriers of* God's archetypal Story of all stories.[11]

All sin is unbelief in the gospel. A gospel coach leads a disciple-leader to recognize idols and then, through repentance, to experience gospel transformation by putting off the old, corrupted, deceitful self and putting on a new self (Ephesians 4:22 – 23). "Change is the norm for everyone," writes Timothy Lane and Paul David Tripp.[12] Church leadership is a stress-filled environment. When we experience stress, we respond toward either good advice or good news. A gospel coach helps a church leader to lean into the only solution to the stress of ministry.

CHAPTER 5

THE THREE ASPECTS FOR EXAMINING LIFE

GOSPEL COACHES CARE FOR CHRISTIAN LEADERS, and in turn, these leaders are freed to shepherd their flocks and to engage in the redemptive mission of the church. One of the core commitments of a coach is to promote the local church as the seat of ministry—the place where community, mission, and the gospel explode in luminescent vibrancy to the world for the glory of God.

A gospel-centered church is focused on seeing the work of Jesus Christ—his life, death, and resurrected life—applied now through the work of the Holy Spirit, bringing transformation to their city, region, and the nations. Through the work of Jesus, God has forgiven his people of their rebellion against him and fills, empowers, and directs them. They are being progressively changed by the ongoing application of God's grace so that they can serve others in love.

THE MESSAGE AND PEOPLE OF THE CHURCH ARE THE HOPE FOR THE WORLD

We believe that the church, both its message and its people, are the hope for the world. The church, as the gathered community of God's people, is the only institution in the world designed and equipped by God for the spiritual, cultural, and social renewal of all nations. We also believe that starting new churches is an effective means for reaching lost people with the gospel. Church planting establishes new, healthy, reproducing groups of believers who are reaching, discipling, and equipping people in their region with the gospel and then releasing them into their local communities to bring their "world" in contact with the transforming power of the kingdom of God. This is God's way of bringing redemptive renewal. Bruce McNichol writes in *Christianity Today* that churches over fifteen years old produce an average of only three converts to Christ per year for every one hundred church members. Churches three years to fifteen years old produce an average of five converts to Christ per year for every one hundred church members. But churches under three years of age produce an average of ten converts to Christ per year for every one hundred church members.[1] That's twice as much as existing churches. I served as a pastor at a Mars Hill Church that gathers within walking distance of the University of Washington in Seattle. In the first four months of this church plant, fifty-one people were baptized. Clearly, a new work often produces new disciples at a much greater rate.

The gospel of Jesus Christ is the ultimate solution to every social, spiritual, cultural, and personal problem. Personal, church, and cultural transformation occurs through a recovery and application of the transforming power of Christ's work and life, through the agency of the Holy Spirit. When we recover the full scope of the gospel story, our churches become places of hope for a runaway world. Why? Because the gospel speaks of our fall into sin, declares what Christ has done to remedy our problem, and then points us to the future renewal of all things—the end of all hunger, poverty, sickness, oppression, injustice, and slavery. This is a hope-filled message! All of the power of sin to destroy and corrupt creation will be replaced with Christ's righteous reign, making all things new and perfect. This is why we pray that God's kingdom will come and that his will will be done, on earth as it is in heaven.

THE MISSION OF JESUS

The mission of the church is the mission of Jesus who was sent by his Father to "seek and to save the lost" (Luke 19:10). The church has been sent into a spiritually broken world to proclaim the good news of redemption that is only made possible by the Son's sacrifice for our sins and the Father's love for us. Just as God sent Jesus on this mission, Jesus now sends every believer on this mission (John 17:14–16, 18; 20:21). We respond to this calling by following Jesus and becoming his fishers of men (Matthew 4:19). When we neglect the calling to make disciples, we neglect the mission of God and cease being a church that is truly "following" Jesus in his mission.

God calls his church to participate in his redemptive mission in the world and in the renewal of all things (Matthew 28:18–20; Acts 1:8). God calls believers of every generation to bring the good news of King Jesus into their cultural context. This involves sharing the gospel message (evangelism), making it known to those who have never heard it and teaching followers of Christ how to incorporate the truth of what God has done into their lives (discipleship). To effectively engage today's culture with the gospel requires the formation of a gospel community that can serve as a visible representation of God's love, a witness to God's work of saving people and transforming their lives through Jesus.

Since we are in Christ, we have a missionary identity. We are adopted into a missionary family. We serve a missionary God. Mission becomes part of our identity, because our Father is a missionary God and we resemble him as children of God. The church is a missionary church with missionary people who do missionary things for the glory of our missionary God. This is who we *are*, but it is also what we *do*. Mission is not something we tack on to a list of optional activities we can choose to do as a Christian. It is at the heart of what we are called and commissioned by Jesus to do, and it is something we must commit ourselves to pursue with all of our abilities. In Matthew 28:18–20, Jesus gives this well-known commission to his disciples, defining their purpose and establishing a clear mandate for them to follow until he returns:

> Jesus came and said to them, "All authority in heaven and on earth has been given to me. Go therefore and make disciples of all nations, baptizing them in the name of the Father and of the Son and of the Holy Spirit, teaching them to observe all that I have commanded you. And behold, I am with you always, to the end of the age."

I served as a lead pastor of three local churches over the course of sixteen years. I never had an opportunity to be coached during this time. While several great things happened and hundreds of people came to saving faith in Christ, much of this came at great expense to my health, my marriage, and my relationships with other people. I never really felt as though I had access to someone who cared for me personally, understood the gospel clearly, and could objectively speak into my life through their own experience and with wisdom from God's Word. For sixteen years I struggled with a great amount of self-inflicted stress. Sometimes it was unbearable. I quietly longed for someone who would listen to me and give me honest, caring feedback, but I was always too proud to ask. So I suffered in silence, released my anger toward those closest to me — including other elders — and was never confronted about any of this, most likely because we were experiencing ongoing numerical growth. But ministry growth is never a good indicator of a church leader's spiritual and emotional health.

Now, both Tom and I are convinced that coaching is the missing practice, the key to making fruitful disciples, equipping leaders, shepherding them to health, and effectively starting new churches. Gospel coaching is based on coaching methods that follow biblical models, yet it adapts to the unique situation the leader faces. It seeks to develop leaders who produce healthy fruit in their lives, not just highly productive doers who can get a job done. It's not a "professional" process whereby a person seeks to sharpen their skills to be successful. It's more of an investment that a coach makes into the life of another leader. A gospel coach invests their knowledge and wisdom but also their love and compassion and personal experience. I've paid professionals to coach me how to succeed in my leadership. And that has value, to be sure. But the real impact on my life — the lasting change that I've experienced — has occurred when that person has combined their professional expertise with an investment of time and care more akin to biblical shepherding. They gave me feedback and direction and offered suggestions for improving the outcome of my ministry, but they also cared for me, held me accountable to my commitments and promises, and pointed out weak areas where my character needed further transformation. As a result, I not only became a better leader in the church; I grew as a husband, father, and friend. A gospel coach cares about the person (heart), imparts truth (head), and offers experiential wisdom (hands).

It is a mistake to separate the *mission* of the church from the *missionaries* of the church, but that is exactly what many churches do today. We judge our effectiveness in the mission by numbers—outward evidence of growth—and consider it a success. But what about those involved in leading that mission? To invest in the mission of the church, we must also invest in our fellow mission bearers, that is, the disciple-leaders all around us. Instead of investing in a program or new concept that can help the church grow, we would be much better off investing in the leaders. In many churches, there are people who attend and are somewhat connected to the ministry, but who often stand around among the other members, not sure if anyone cares, if anyone can help them, or if anyone really knows how to follow Jesus and his mission. Leaders are bombarded with distractions—responding to e-mails, doing administrative work, reading the wrong books, monitoring their social media sites, and pouring time into unmotivated counselees, all when they should be investing their lives into the other leaders around them.

It takes time and energy to equip people to become disciples of Jesus. We should not forget that at the heart of Jesus' ministry plan was the time he spent, nearly three years, walking every day with a small group of twelve men. Through them, he unleashed his plan to change the world. Jesus didn't start with the cream of the crop either. He started with twelve selfish, sinful men who often argued with each other, were impulsive, and frequently lacked faith. Jesus knew that to accomplish the mission God had sent him to do, he had to invest his life, his love, his time, and his words into other men who would be willing to proclaim the good news of his accomplished work of redemption to every nation, tribe, people, and tongue, even at great personal cost (Revelation 7:9).

In Robert Coleman's classic book *The Master Plan of Evangelism*, he comments that Jesus' "basic philosophy is so different from that of the modern church that its implications are nothing less than revolutionary ... [Jesus'] concern was not with programs to reach the multitudes but with men whom the multitudes would follow." Coleman concludes that "men were to be [Jesus'] method of winning the world to God."[2] Following the example of Jesus' leadership means coaching disciple-leaders who will actively pursue the mission of God through the church.

Jesus focused his effort on coaching the Twelve because he was preparing them for a great mission. His preparation was more than a series of lectures; it was a three-year process of life-on-life coaching dealing with personal character, missional skill, and continual spiritual realignment. This process for development involved at least four phases. First, Jesus invited his followers to *come and see* (John 1:39). Next, his invitation moved to *come and follow me* (Mark 1:17). He then asked them to *come and be with me* (Matthew 11:28). In his final phase of coaching, Jesus commanded them to *go to the nations and make disciples* and plant new churches. He empowered his followers with the Holy Spirit and promised to be with them always, commanding them to follow his example in teaching and producing new disciples (Matthew 28:18–20).

In the illustration below (Figure 7), we see our coaching diagram further clarified with the addition of three categories in which a coach must intentionally invest: the personal, spiritual, and missional aspects of the disciple-leader's life. The gospel is communicated and modeled to a person, and the outcome is a God-glorifying life. A gospel coach carefully and lovingly examines a person's personal life, spiritual life, and missional life and offers godly counsel that is appropriate for the person and situation.

Gospel coaching facilitates transformation through realignment in the gospel. We can only be truly free when we live in accordance

Figure 7: Three Aspects for Examination in Coaching

So Jesus said to the Jews who had believed in him, "If you abide in my word, you are truly my disciples, and you will know the truth, and the truth will set you free." They answered him, "We are offspring of Abraham and have never been enslaved to anyone. How is it that you say, 'You will become free'?"

Jesus answered them, "Truly, truly, I say to you, everyone who commits sin is a slave to sin. The slave does not remain in the house forever; the son remains forever. So if the Son sets you free, you will be free indeed."

—*John 8:31–36*

with the truth of God's Word. The gospel of grace is the path of life we walk along to find life transformation. The gospel is the ultimate solution for every problem and issue we face and is obviously something outside of ourselves. We must go to Christ to get it. It is the supernatural power of God graciously given to us by his Spirit.

The greatest benefit a gospel coach can provide disciple-leaders is guidance in applying the gospel in each challenge or opportunity personally, spiritually, and missionally. The gospel coach and disciple-leader enter into a supportive relationship that leads to continual gospel renewal and character deepening and results in the disciple following Jesus faithfully for the glory of God, the good of others, and the joy of serving him.

THREE ASPECTS OF OUR LIVES AS BELIEVERS

Wayne Grudem describes a healthy church as one that has upward, inward, and outward characteristics. We believe this is also true of our lives as individual believers. The following diagram (Figure 8) illustrates these three aspects of a person's life and the interplay among them. None of these aspects can be partitioned from the others. The personal affects the spiritual; the spiritual life affects the missional life; the missional life affects the spiritual life and the personal life.

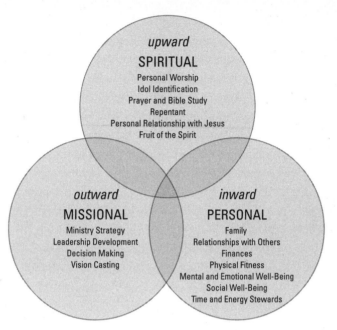

Figure 8: Three Interrelated Aspects

SPIRITUAL ASPECTS

The upward characteristics — or *spiritual aspects* — deal with our worship and praise of God and our belief in his promises to do good for us. He is our love, joy, and adoration — the one we worship with all of our heart. These aspects are expressed in our prayers, study of the Bible, and meditations. We worship God by dedicating our time, resources, and skills to his glory. A gospel coach asks about the disciple's personal worship, his prayer life, and his demonstration of the fruit of the Spirit. The coach examines a disciple-leader's personal relationship with Jesus, how well the disciple is repenting of sin, and their commitment to a gospel community.

I was recently coaching a pastor, and after asking questions about his personal life, he told me he was feeling depressed. I wasn't surprised, as I've found that both depression and anger are quite common among pastors today. I could have responded to his depression by examining his diet and exercise regimen or talking with him about his schedule and how much time off he was taking. We could have explored the medical reasons for his feeling this way. I could have focused on his work—on his management of the staff and volunteer leaders. Instead, I probed a bit to learn why he was experiencing this depression. He shared that he felt he was no longer fulfilling all that he believed God wanted him to accomplish. It was obvious that his depression was really a spiritual issue, so I helped him to explore his identity in Christ. We talked about his perceived need to succeed, to raise the attendance of the church higher than the nearly one thousand people currently coming to his church (after only a short time of ministering there). Though his depression was first uncovered through a *personal* inquiry, we quickly began examining it through a *spiritual* lens, and he readily repented of the value his idol of success was bringing to him. He openly acknowledged that his perceived lack of success was contributing to his depression. Interestingly, a year later his church experienced over 50 percent growth, approaching two thousand attendees.

"The heart is the command center for every battle," writes Dr. Bryan Chapell. "A full and consistent apprehension of why we love God is the most effective piece of armor in the Christian arsenal, because the Devil always begins his attack with an alienation of our affections. Thus our most powerful spiritual weapon is consistent adulation of the mercy of God revealed in Christ."[3] There are many problems and challenges that we face in our lives that can't be addressed by problem solving or skill development. We can only be strong when we are in the Lord and under his mighty power. I find it disturbing to see how many spiritual issues we try to address with a physical tool. We may try to use silence and solitude, prayer and fasting, Sabbath rhythms and memorization of Scripture, as techniques in an attempt to address spiritual problems. We sometimes believe that rubbing the genie's lamp of spiritual disciplines will provide the solution for the void in our heart. In some cases, this approach leads to pride and self-reliance as we become more outwardly disciplined. Instead, we have to address the alienation of our heart from pursuing a relationship with our holy, loving God. I've seen far too many church leaders whose hearts were far from God but who were "successfully" serving others, even though they knew they didn't love

God as much as they loved themselves, their position, and their sinful desires.

PERSONAL ASPECTS

Examining the personal aspects (inward characteristics) of a person's life leads to a focus on a disciple's understanding of their identity in Christ; their relationships with others; service to others; family issues; finances; physical fitness; mental, emotional, and social wellness; time management; and academic pursuits.

I (Scott) knew two pastors who committed suicide, and in both cases they did not have other people in their lives regularly asking them about their personal and spiritual lives. Both were seemingly very successful in their church and in accomplishing the work of ministry. Both were strong leaders. They spoke, wrote, and coached other pastors, sharing their wisdom on how to effectively lead a church plant. But after they took their own lives, we learned that both of them had been deeply troubled for several years. One of them had marital struggles, and no one had known the full extent of the problem. When his marriage was not restored to his satisfaction, he horrifically took his own life in front of his wife. The other pastor had a carefully hidden addiction to sleeping pills, and again, no one had known. After he lost his job after mishandling the church finances, he was found dead. The state medical examiner declared his overdose of sleeping pills to be a suicide. Both of these shepherds had friends and consultants, but they did not avail themselves of gospel shepherds to openly talk about their years of chronic pain, the layers of marital problems, the addictions, and the underlying anger and fear they felt. When we only judge the health of a leader by outward signs of success, we are in danger of making a tragic mistake.

As mentioned earlier, most church leaders are overwhelmed by the work of ministry. Much of the reason we started the gospel coach program was out of a genuine concern for the souls of pastors. I recently spoke to the widow of one of the pastors who had committed suicide, and it was a sobering moment. She shared that her husband didn't just come home one day and explode. Instead, she said, "It was as if his soul had slowly faded out—just like that song by Casting Crowns":[4]

> It's a slow fade when black and white have turned to gray.
> Thoughts invade, choices are made, a price will be paid.
> When you give yourself away. People never crumble in a day.[5]

This pastor's widow then urged me to tell pastors they should seek the help they need before allowing this kind of tragedy to happen. She admitted that it was her husband's pride that often kept him from letting others know about the chronic pain that had existed for years in his soul. His pride had simply masked great fears that he had wrestled with all of his life. But no one had really known about his troubled soul—until it was too late.

INDICATORS OF A TROUBLED SOUL

As the apostle Paul shared with the Ephesian elders before leaving them, it is essential that we learn how to "pay careful attention" to our own hearts and to the behavior and emotional signs of those in our care: "Pay careful attention to yourselves and to all the flock, in which the Holy Spirit has made you overseers, to care for the church of God, which he obtained with his own blood" (Acts 20:28).

When dealing with the personal aspects—the inward life of a person that is often hidden from sight—we have to be on the lookout for signs of a slowly fading soul. Over the years, I have learned to recognize the following indicators of souls that might be troubled by personal problems and struggles:

- minimal longing for Jesus
- minimal joy and gladness
- minimal dependence on God
- maximal thoughts of self
- maximal burdens of ministry
- maximal outbursts of anger (masked fear)

HELP FOR TROUBLED SOULS

How do you coach someone who exhibits one or more of these indicators? While the following is far from an exhaustive list, we offer these eight suggestions for you to pass on to those whose souls are troubled:

1. *Renew your mind with prolonged Scripture reading.* Church leaders need to stop treating God's Word as a piece of literature. One of the first and most basic steps to take is to reaffirm that your reading of Scripture is time spent with a loving God who is speaking to you personally. The psalmist David wrote, "I have set the LORD always before me; because he is at my right hand, I shall not be shaken. Therefore my heart is glad, and my whole being rejoices; my flesh also dwells secure" (Psalm 16:8–9). The apostle Paul encouraged the church at Corinth, "So we do not lose heart. Though our outer nature is wasting away, our inner nature is being renewed day by day" (2 Corinthians 4:16). Personal renewal comes through both reading and heeding God's Word.

2. *Pray with an unhurried heart.* Pray without rushing through a list or a formula for praying. Let God speak slowly to your heart. Allow yourself to sit quietly beside the still waters. Stop your perpetual motion, and just sit with God and talk. He might have something to say to you if you stop long enough to listen. You might find you are even more inclined to pray *to* God, not just *about* God when you are hurting.

3. *Confess the hidden sins of your heart.* God is after your heart, your thoughts, and your deepest desires. Peter writes, "Let your adorning be the hidden person of the heart with the imperishable beauty of a gentle and quiet spirit, which in God's sight is very precious" (1 Peter 3:4). You may be troubled because your heart is full of unconfessed sin. Spend some time in honest reflection, asking the Holy Spirit to bring conviction to your heart and reveal unconfessed sin. Then acknowledge your sin and confirm your identify in Christ by declaring the gospel, preaching it to yourself.

4. *Live in true community with others, and allow them to truly know you.* How many people actually know you—the private person, not the public person? Do they know about

your finances, your marriage, your anger, and your sins? You need others to help you in your battle against sin (Hebrews 3:12–13). Paul David Tripp said that without a community, we are prone to listen to our own lies and buy into our own delusions.[6] Find trusted friends who can listen to your struggles.

5. *Review your calling by God.* In his book *The Call,* Os Guinness writes, "Calling is the truth that God calls us to himself so decisively that everything we are, everything we do, and everything we have is invested with a special devotion and dynamism lived out as a response to his summons and service."[7] Later he states, "The notion of calling is vital to each of us because it touches on the modern search for a basis for individual identity and an understanding of humanness itself."[8] Guinness goes on to point to the necessity of addressing the deepest questions—Who am I? and Why am I alive? Calling is not a synonym for a comfortable life, but it acts as a compass when we are lost.

6. *Review the goals and steps of action you have for your life.* You may have impossible goals, or you may lack a practical strategy to fulfill them. Both of them need to be reviewed regularly. Church leaders waste huge amounts of time on things that have nothing to do with their calling or goals. View your life in terms of whole-life stewardship for the glory of God.

7. *Review the way you are managing your whole life.* Your life may feel out of control because it *is* out of control. You may need to take inventory of your time, your relationships, your finances, and your health in order to accomplish the goals you have for your life.

8. *Rest in God's grace, love and acceptance of you.* You don't have to earn God's love and acceptance. Through the grace of God and the sacrifice of Jesus, God has imputed to you Christ's righteousness and you are a beloved son in whom God is well pleased. You can't earn more favor from God than you have right now. Because you are a child of God,

he doesn't demand anything more than the substitutionary atonement of his Son, Jesus Christ, to declare you righteous.

MISSIONAL ASPECTS

We've intentionally emphasized the spiritual and personal aspects of a person's life before the missional aspects because it is our natural tendency to judge by outward appearances. But as mentioned at the outset of this chapter, it is a mistake to separate the mission of the church from the missionaries of the church. These outward, missional aspects of a leader's life deal with them knowing and embracing God's love for sinners. To truly grasp the necessity of the missional aspects, it is helpful to understand God's call to be light and salt in the world. This includes not only our calling but our investment of time, energy, and money for the kingdom; our leadership in local ministry; developing leaders; and living a missionary lifestyle in one's community.

An effective coach will diagnose the ministry competence and commitment of the disciple to this mission. As the disciple progresses in his competence and commitment, they must assume more of the initiative in this missional responsibility. A coach remains involved in this aspect of a disciple-leader's life by continuing to raise the level of the disciple's competence and commitment to their primary ministry responsibility.

Four basic styles of coaching can be utilized depending on the situation, experience, and need of the disciple-leader:

1. *Exhorting Style.* For disciples with minimal competence and commitment, a coach should use a more structured approach while still urging responsibility and ownership toward the disciple. In this style, the coach would assist in setting goals, guide the disciple to develop a plan for their ministry and life, provide direction on how to accomplish their goal, evaluate the disciple's progress closely, and hold the disciple accountable for their decisions.

2. *Edifying Style.* When a disciple has increased in his competence and commitment, the coach can use an approach that provides a great deal of relational support while continuing

to engage in dialogue with the disciple. The coach reviews the disciple's goals, monitors the progress of their soul, explores implementation plans, and provides feedback and encouragement.

3. *Enabling Style.* When the disciple's skills are reasonably well developed but motivation is still needed, the enabling style is appropriate. The coach should provide considerable support but not a great deal of specific direction. The coach monitors goal setting, seeks clarification on steps of action, encourages the disciple to make bold decisions, helps solve problems, and provides encouragement and support.

4. *Empowering Style.* When disciples display maturity in their competence and commitment, a coach implements the empowering style. The coach offers assistance in reviewing goals and plans of the disciple in ministry responsibilities. The coach affirms decisions made by the disciple, provides feedback for changes and adjustments, and continues to affirm wise decision making by the disciple.[9]

When asking questions about the missional aspects of the disciple, the coach needs to determine which issues are of greatest importance to help a disciple to pursue God's calling in his life. Is it a skill or an experience issue (hands), a knowledge issue (head), or a motivational or character issue (heart)? Rather than allowing the disciple-leader to solely determine the direction of the coaching session — the approach that is most common in a client-centered coaching environment — a gospel coach should provide ministry-specific coaching when probing the missional aspects of the disciple. It is advantageous to the leader and the local church where the leader serves to identify the goals and steps of action God has placed on him and then agree on a plan to fulfill it.

GOSPEL COACHING IN THREE ASPECTS OF LIFE

As we said before, gospel coaching is a relational process of shepherding a disciple-leader in her personal, spiritual, and missional life for the good of the leader, the fruitfulness of the mission, and the glory of God. A gospel-centered approach to coaching a disciple-leader is necessary in all three aspects of life. In our experience of working with church leaders, we have found that a gospel approach is important because it most directly affects the personal growth of the disciple. For this to be effective, a coach must himself know, live in, and live out the gospel of Jesus Christ. A coaching relationship will shrivel if the coach is not practicing what they share and teach. When there is common agreement about the necessity of the gospel, however, you'll find that great chemistry often develops between a coach and their disciple-leader.

Second, the disciple-leader also needs to focus on continuously understanding and working out the implications of the gospel message in their own personal life as a Christ-follower and as a leader in the church. Leading a ministry is an excellent context for learning about your personal weaknesses, your struggles with idolatry and selfishness, and the great power of the gospel to change and transform our hearts. Each one of us is blind to our own limitations. If a leader wishes to faithfully serve a church body, the gospel must first change them. They need to develop a comprehensive gospel-centered framework for thinking about, evaluating, and doing personal ministry.

Third, the disciple-leader needs to learn and apply the gospel for their own missional growth. In developing other leaders in the community of believers, a disciple-leader learns to appropriate and apply the gospel with others they are leading. Reproducing other leaders is one of the most important tasks of a church leader. They will have no greater privilege than to reproduce leaders who have clearly understood the rich theology of the gospel and are applying gospel dynamics to their lives and ministries and surrounding communities.

Believers in their missional focus to the city, to the lost, and to the poor and needy will need a mixture of humility and courage. Humility allows Christians to openly confess their sins to nonbelievers, and courage enables them to repent and receive grace. These evidences of genuine humility may compel those you serve to see the beauty of Christ and his love rather than stealing his glory for themselves. Application of the gospel in mission will drive the believers to love and serve their neighbors (rather than using their neighbors) and extend courageous acts of mercy and evangelism. Believers should respect nonbelievers without fearing them or disdaining them.

Finally, a disciple-leader needs gospel-centered coaching to promote spiritual growth in the community of believers. Every single area of a believer's life needs to be considered in light of the gospel, and this includes relationships with others. The gospel creates a new kind of community—one that is built on grace, compassion, humility, love, and faith. A disciple-leader will teach, motivate, recruit volunteers, raise funds, and lead and counsel, all in light of the gospel. Martin Luther wrote the following:

> Here I must take counsel of the gospel. I must hearken to the gospel, which teacheth me, not what I ought to do (for that is the proper office of the law), but what Jesus Christ the Son of God hath done for me: to wit, that he suffered and died to deliver me from sin and death. The gospel willeth me to receive this, and to believe it. And this is the truth of the gospel. It is also the principal article of all Christian doctrine ... Most necessary it is, therefore, that we should know this article well, teach it unto others and beat it into their heads continually.[10]

It is essential that a coach knows the gospel and that the leader they disciple is wrestling with its implications in their own life. And ultimately, the process of gospel coaching will affect the way a leader leads in the community of faith. It will encourage them to begin thinking about the gospel in every area of life, working it inside and out and beating it into the heads of others if necessary. Since leading a church is a spiritual endeavor, a gospel friendship between coach and disciple is ultimately a vital element that every church needs in order to effectively live out their calling as they wrestle with the implications of the gospel in their own community.

PART 2

COACHING LIKE A SHEPHERD-LEADER

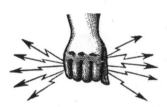

CHAPTER 6

CHURCH LEADERSHIP IS SHEPHERDING

MODERN CHURCH LEADERS certainly have no lack of leadership models to draw from. We've heard the church leader described as a CEO, coach, mentor, conductor, guide, servant, and soldier—to name just a few. But the most common description of a church leader in the Bible is that of a *shepherd*. When most people think of shepherds, they picture either gentle young men playing flutes and clad in flowing robes or—worse yet—Little Bo Peep searching for her lost sheep. Given the problematic cultural images associated with the term *shepherd*, one prominent Christian leader has suggested that the term should be abandoned today. Though it served as an effective model of leadership in biblical times, he claims that it is simply not applicable to today's church culture.

Needless to say, we strongly disagree. Leading a church entails feeding, attending, and keeping a flock. It is depicted in the Bible with the Greek verb *poimainō*, which is translated by words such as "shepherd," "care," "rule," and "tend." Paul told the Ephesian elders to care (*poimainō*) for the church of God (Acts 20:28). Along with the verb, we also find the noun *poimēn* (poy-mane), which is commonly translated as both "pastor" (Ephesians 4:11) and "shepherd." Jesus uses this word to refer to a shepherd in 1 Peter 2:25, "You were straying like sheep, but have now returned to the Shepherd [*poimēn*] and Overseer of your souls." In other words, you cannot pastor without shepherding. You cannot image the "great Shepherd [*poimēn*] of the sheep" (Hebrews 13:20) without shepherding your flock (*poimnē*, Luke 2:8).

In his book *Shepherds after My Own Heart*, Timothy Laniak notes that as church leaders in the modern world, we tend to naturally view ourselves as executives of a corporation rather than as shepherds.[1] But the question is not which image we find most attractive. Ultimately, the shepherd image is the one that must dominate our church leadership paradigm because it reflects the Bible's teaching on leadership. If we abandon the shepherd imagery of the Scriptures, we will lose the uniqueness of the Bible's teaching on leadership, leaving us with dangerously unbiblical models of leadership defined by the values and goals of the corporate world.

Biblical church leadership and gospel coaching are, at heart, shepherding. God promised, "I will give you shepherds after my own heart, who will feed you with knowledge and understanding" (Jeremiah 3:15). God uses shepherding metaphors repeatedly in Scripture to describe leadership among God's people. The prophets Jeremiah, Ezekiel, and Isaiah refer to Israel's leaders as either good shepherds or wicked shepherds. Moses and Aaron (Psalm 77:20), Zechariah (Zechariah 10:2), and David (1 Samuel 17:34-35) were shepherds. Yahweh God reveals himself as the true shepherd ruler of Israel (Psalm 23; 95:6–7). The coming King of Israel, Jesus, is prophesied to be a shepherd who tends a flock and gathers the lambs in his arms (Isaiah 40:11). The gospel of Matthew depicts Jesus as the compassionate Davidic shepherd (Matthew 2:6; see also 25:31–32). Mark shows Jesus as a shepherd (Mark 6:34; 14:27). Luke reveals Jesus as the seeking and saving shepherd (Luke 15:1–7; 19:10), while John's gospel portrays Jesus as both the self-sacrificing shepherd (John 10) and the Passover Lamb (John 1:29).

In the late 1970s and early 1980s, the Shepherding Movement emphasized submission to a personal pastor or shepherd, and subsequently the practice brought accusations of authoritarianism. This is not what is being presented here. The key leaders in the Shepherding Movement later issued a statement of concern and regret for how their principles had been "handled in an immature way."[2]

Gospel coaching seeks to humbly capture the biblical principles of shepherd leadership while remaining under the authority and reign of the chief Shepherd, Jesus Christ (1 Peter 5:4). In the following chapters, we will take a closer look at Scripture and unpack ten qualities of a gospel coach. When we grasp the truth that biblical church leadership is shepherding as an "undershepherd" of the chief Shepherd, Jesus Christ, it sharpens our leadership and produces a healthier flock.

Gospel coaching is a process for responsibly and passionately caring for others that is based on the biblical model of shepherding. A gospel coach shepherds those people in their charge, that is, those whom God has entrusted to them to exercise oversight for the well-being of their souls.[3] While the primary instruction in the verses in 1 Peter 5 relates specifically to the office of elder, a secondary application can be extended to all leaders who exercise spiritual oversight under the authority of local church oversight — elders, deacons, small group leaders, associate pastors, teachers, and women's ministry directors.

> So I exhort the elders among you, as a fellow elder and a witness of the sufferings of Christ, as well as a partaker in the glory that is going to be revealed: shepherd the flock of God that is among you, exercising oversight, not under compulsion, but willingly, as God would have you; not for shameful gain, but eagerly; not domineering over those in your charge, but being examples to the flock.
>
> —1 Peter 5:1–3

Peter lays out four key characteristics that define gospel friendship — the basis of the shepherding relationship.

1. *A gospel coach gives a reproducible example to those they are discipling.* "Shepherd the flock ... not domineering over those in your charge, but being *examples* to the flock" (1 Peter 5:2–3, emphasis added). Jesus provided a pattern for his disciples to follow. He did not control their actions. He

modeled worshipful obedience to the mission of God. As leaders, we are undershepherds—submissive agents of our chief Shepherd, Jesus Christ. Making disciples is the mission of the church, and it includes relating to unbelieving neighbors, family, and friends with close enough proximity for them to observe us "imaging" God before their very eyes, and joining forces with other believers to bring community within the context of daily living. It is an ordinary life lived with extraordinary gospel intentionality.

2. *A gospel coach recognizes their own identity as a sheep in need of a shepherd.* Coaches do not lead and disciple leaders because they have something unique or special to offer. The glory of God is what motivates this interaction; "as a *fellow elder* and a witness of the sufferings of Christ, as well as a partaker in the glory that is going to be revealed" (1 Peter 5:1, emphasis added). A gospel coach is first and foremost a believer who recognizes that they, too, are laboring for the King alongside others who are also in need of God's grace and mercy. They are simultaneously a shepherd *and* a sheep. Often, coaches must fight as wounded soldiers, aware of their own painful circumstances but continuing to fight and stand up for the sake of others and finish the mission they have been given.

3. *A gospel coach initiates relationships with the people immediately around them.* God has placed each of us in relationships in which we can care for those around us. We do not have to look too far to find people whom God is calling us to lead and serve. They are all around us—in our homes, our neighborhoods, our offices, our classrooms, and our church. "Shepherd the flock of God that is *among you*, exercising oversight" (1 Peter 5:2, emphasis added). People have a natural tendency to wander away into isolation. But a sheep left alone will starve to death, be ravaged by wolves, or wander into fatal danger. "All we like sheep have gone astray; we have turned—every one—to his own way" (Isaiah 53:6). Gospel coaches seek out the people God has called them

to serve, who are in their midst, inviting them out of their isolation and potential danger to a relationship of safety.

4. *A gospel coach initiates caring acts of service for others*: "not under compulsion, but willingly, as God would have you" (1 Peter 5:2). In the gospel of John, Jesus talked about a shepherd who abandoned his sheep when trouble arose: "He who is a hired hand and not a shepherd, who does not own the sheep, sees the wolf coming and leaves the sheep and flees, and the wolf snatches them and scatters them. He flees because he is a hired hand and cares nothing for the sheep" (John 10:12–13). In our self-centeredness, we often discard people in our lives without giving it much thought. We reason that if we are not being forced to care for them or paid to care for them ("not for shameful gain" [1 Peter 5:2]), we do not have to shepherd them through their difficulties because it is simply too costly and may offer us nothing in return. Our motive for coaching is not personal gain or a sense of guilty compulsion; it is a willingness to sacrificially serve that comes from a heart rooted in the gospel of God's sacrificial love.

There is perhaps no more famous shepherd in the Bible than David. God chose David the young shepherd boy and took him from the sheepfolds, from following the nursing ewes, and raised him up to shepherd the people of Israel. Psalm 78:70–72 tells us that David shepherded and guided them with his skillful hand. Shepherd leadership in the church displays Jesus' love for us and our validity as his disciples (John 13:34–35). When we love one another with this kind of brotherly affection, we make a commitment to care for others and be cared for by others, to fight for others and to be fought for by others. We must take the biblical model of the shepherd leader seriously and initiate true community with those whom God entrusts to us as disciples and then stand by their side and fight for the glory of God.

Ultimately all of us are Jesus' own sheep, and he is leading us to himself. As leaders and undershepherds, our job is to lead those in our care to King Jesus and not to any other undershepherd. To lose sight of Jesus in shepherding others is to miss the point entirely. Elders are assigned by the Holy Spirit to care for the souls of those in their flock, those under their charge. But others in the church help to extend the elders' care by overseeing smaller communities, groups, or individual people. Regardless of your particular role, it is important that those who are called to shepherd others take this divine assignment seriously, pointing those in your charge to the great Shepherd of their souls, Jesus Christ.

We believe that this shepherding model is one of the best ways to explain how we followers of Jesus can continue our Lord's knowing, feeding, leading, and protective work. As it is with all that we do, we must remember that our work is only possible because of his atoning life and death, whereby he overcame our sin ignorance, our guilt, and our corruption. Jesus provides us with illumination, redemption, and hope as we serve disciple-leaders by shepherding them through the joys and challenges of life, ministry, and growth in the Lord. In the next section, we'll break this down into even more practical application steps, detailing the specifics of what types of questions to ask and how to schedule and organize good gospel conversations.

What does it mean to be a shepherd? There are several ways of looking at the key roles that a shepherd has in caring for their sheep. We believe that at the heart of gospel coaching are four key shepherding principles. A shepherd must:

1. know the sheep
2. feed the sheep
3. lead the sheep
4. protect the sheep

These four principles not only form the basis for your own gospel coaching of disciple-leaders; they are four key areas of accountability as you spend time together. The following chapters explain how a gospel coach does this as an image of the chief Shepherd.

CHAPTER 7

COACHING QUALITIES: KNOWING

CAN ANYONE BECOME AN EFFECTIVE COACH? I have had several athletic coaches over the years. Some were very good coaches, and others were not effective. As an athletic coach myself for many years, I've often thought about what enables some coaches to get their teams to perform to their full potential. Generally, both effective and ineffective athletic coaches understand the technicalities of the game. The difference is that ineffective coaches don't seem to get the most out of their players.

Legendary basketball coach John Wooden died at the age of ninety-nine in 2010. His accomplishments in basketball are unmatched by any other men's college basketball coach. He coached UCLA to an eighty-eight game winning streak and they won a record ten NCAA national championships in an amazing twelve-year period. Coach Wooden once said that he made his living as a coach but lived his life to be a mentor. He was himself constantly being mentored by others. Wooden said that a mentor (coach) was an individual who models life principles. A mentor teaches about humility, contentment, interactions with family and friends, and keeping our priorities straight in a world that often threatens to invert them. He said that a mentor (coach) will encourage others as well as correct them when they move away from a healthy lifestyle. Wooden said it is not enough to just find a mentor; it's every bit as important to become one yourself.[1] Many of these elements fit well with our understanding of the role of a gospel coach.

Is coaching, then, something that anyone can learn? The ultimate outcome of coaching is to glorify God by paying careful attention to a disciple-leader's personal, spiritual, and missional life. A disciple should display evidence of God's love and have a passion to worship God, engaging in a life-on-life relationship with other disciples and witnessing to the resurrected glorious Savior to a dying world.

But to be effective, gospel coaches must first reflect the gospel themselves. Humans were created in God's image so that we might represent God, like ambassadors to a foreign country represent their country.[2] When we find our identity in Jesus, we become image bearers (mirror images) of the life-giving God of the Bible. Bearing his image means taking the opportunity to image God with our surrendered wills. We do this by being renewed daily in the image of Christ (Colossians 3:10) and reflecting back in praise to the Father, Son, and Holy Spirit. We image God when we reflect or mirror God's thinking, when we love what God loves, when we grieve over the things that grieve God, when we mirror the mercy and comfort God has shown us. We are called to reflect the light of Jesus. Techniques for coaching will not override the coach's lack of a personal relationship with Jesus Christ. Coaches cannot merely tell their disciples what to do; they must walk out in front of them as examples. Disciples need to hear the passion in their prayers. They need to see the passion in their actions and in their focus.

TEN QUALITIES OF A GOSPEL COACH

We have outlined the four shepherding roles of knowing, feeding, leading, and protecting the sheep. In this chapter, we will define the ten qualities of an effective coach, joining together the four shepherding dimensions, and then we will unpack the first quality. A coach brings all of the issues, questions, needs, problems, and solutions into orbit around a gospel dynamic that is applied to each situation, because the gospel is the ultimate solution for every problem a disciple faces. An effective coach will exhibit each of these ten qualities as they engage in the four roles of shepherding:

Shepherding Roles	Qualities of a Gospel Coach
Know the sheep	1. Relating personally
Feed the sheep	2. Nourishing with truth 3. Inspiring toward Jesus 4. Equipping in needs
Lead the sheep	5. Investing sacrificially 6. Overseeing every aspect of a person's life 7. Guiding with Spirit-empowered discernment
Protect the sheep	8. Displaying compassion 9. Comforting with hope in the gospel 10. Fighting for their good

Table 4: Qualities of a Gospel Coach

KNOW THE SHEEP

> ### Know: Develop a personal relationship.

Sheep know the shepherd to whom they belong. They are named, known, and counted every day.[3] Naming usually takes place soon after birth, especially if there is some distinguishing characteristic. Naming is a powerful, tangible expression of the shepherd's intimate bond that begins at birth and grows through an animal's tenure with the flock. That is why it was so significant when Jesus said, "I am the good shepherd. I know my own and my own know me, just as the Father knows me and I know the Father; and I lay down my life for the sheep … My sheep hear my voice, and I know them, and they follow me" (John 10:14–15, 27). We can't expect someone to follow our lead if we don't have a relationship with them.

The grace of God found in the gospel story invites us to become vulnerable with others with whom we have a relationship. Without Christ, we have a natural aversion to vulnerability, to "being known." A coaching friendship grounded in trust and grace can be a powerful influence for a disciple-leader. A disciple-leader deliberately sits under the influence of another, submitting to the coach's strengths and being exposed to the coach's weaknesses. The disciple intentionally chooses to let the coach know them and have access into their personal, spiritual, and missional life.

Having an intimate relationship with God is the most foundational of all relationships. Exodus 6:7 reads, "I will take you to be my people, and I will be your God, and you shall know that I am the LORD your God, who has brought you out from under the burdens of the Egyptians." Psalm 100:3 assures us, "Know that the LORD, he is God! It is he who made us, and we are his; we are his people, and the sheep of his pasture."

Jesus provided a way for us to know God personally through Jesus' life, death, burial, and resurrection. Jesus declared, "I am the way, and the truth, and the life. No one comes to the Father except through me. If you had known me, you would have known my Father also. From now on you do know him and have seen him" (John 14:6–7). Timothy Witmer, a professor of practical theology at Westminster Theological Seminary, states, "It is our restored, loving relationship with the Lord that flows over into transforming our relationships with other people, particularly those who are also part of his flock."[4] The first phase in gospel coaching is connecting relationally with your disciple-leader. Knowing the person you are coaching is necessary in order to effectively lead and counsel them. The coach comes alongside the disciple as a friend, comforter, and guide.

We are exhorted in 1 Peter 5:2-3 to intimately know those who are under our care. The Holy Spirit has allotted and entrusted to us specific people whom we are to know and shepherd. The phrase translated "those in your charge" in 1 Peter 5:3 ("those allotted to your charge" [NASB]; "those entrusted to you" [NIV]) comes from the Greek word *klēros*. According to scholars, "In classical Greek, *klēros* was an allotment of land assigned to a citizen by the civic authorities, the distribution frequently being made by lot."[5] Timothy Laniak applies this understanding to the church, suggesting "the use of *klēros*, found most frequently in the Septuagint ... suggests that the 'real estate' in the new community is the people themselves, clustered under caring guardians."[6] In other words, God has allotted and assigned people to each of us—those individuals he wants us to coach and shepherd.

As we recognize that it is the Holy Spirit who has made us over-seers of others' lives (Acts 20:28) and that God has entrusted us with and assigned us his sheep to know and to care for their souls, we are inclined to shepherd soberly and faithfully. When trouble arises, we must avoid the temptation to abandon our sheep or seek greener pastures with smarter/cooler/nicer sheep to shepherd. We must rest in the confidence that God is at work and that the troubles we face are an opportunity to depend on him and to see him honored and glorified in this relationship.

Because shepherding involves a personal relationship with specific people placed under our care by God himself, we must intentionally seek to know them personally, extensively, and intimately. Dr. Bob Logan, a church-planting coach for over twenty years and the founder of CoachNet Global, says that a foundation of trust, care, and mutual respect is ultimately dependent on three questions that a disciple asks himself about his coach: (1) Can I trust you? (2) Do you care? (3) Can you help?[7] The only way to answer these is by knowing one another relationally.

In his classic book *Reformed Pastor*, Richard Baxter (c. 1615–1691) suggests the following:

> We must labor to be acquainted, not only with the persons, but with the state of all people ... what are the sins of which they are most in danger, and what duties are they most apt to neglect, and what temptations they are most liable to; for if we know not their temperament or disease, we are not likely to prove successful physicians.[8]

A coach has the greatest influence over those he knows best. In a gospel coaching relationship, *knowing the disciple* is the first step to develop a common relationship that will lead to passionately pursuing God's calling for the disciple.

Jesus said that a good shepherd knows his sheep, and his sheep knows his voice. A relationship is imperative in leadership:

> "The sheep hear his voice, and he calls his own sheep by name and leads them out. When he has brought out all his own, he goes before them, and the sheep follow him, for they know his

voice. A stranger they will not follow, but they will flee from him, for they do not know the voice of strangers ...

"I am the good shepherd. I know my own and my own know me, just as the Father knows me and I know the Father; and I lay down my life for the sheep. And I have other sheep that are not of this fold. I must bring them also, and they will listen to my voice. So there will be one flock, one shepherd ...

"My sheep hear my voice, and I know them, and they follow me."

—John 10:3–5, 14–16, 27

The coach relates to the disciple-leader with mutual knowledge that develops trust and followership. Why is it that some athletic coaches are not able to get the most out of their players? I once told a basketball coach who was struggling through a losing season that I didn't think his players were willing to sacrifice for him on the court, and as a result, they were not motivated to excel. The players didn't care because they had confided to me that they lacked a personal relationship with their coach. The coach disagreed with my analysis—and his team lost repeatedly to less talented teams! As we coach, we must always do it in a relational manner. Those we disciple must know that we care about them. We cannot effectively lead someone without relating to them personally.

We see in John 10 that the sheep won't follow strangers and will in fact run from them. When we attempt to lead a disciple with whom we have built no relationship, it should not surprise us that we are met with resistance and fear. What may appear on the surface as a hard-hearted disciple may in fact be a disciple who lacks a meaningful relationship with the coach.

Christ is our friend (John 15:15). We must approach all of our coaching in the context of a relational friend, not just as a consultant or an expert. Coaching is a conversation, not a lecture. The coaching conversation includes listening, observing, responding, interacting, equipping, supporting, encouraging, and giving advice. Coaching is an intentional gospel conversation among friends with focused discussions about a disciple's personal, spiritual, and missional life.

A personal relationship is foundational to effective coaching experiences that also include feeding the disciple-leader with truth.

CHAPTER 8

COACHING QUALITIES: FEEDING

FEED THE SHEEP

> Feed: Provide spiritual nourishment and truth.

Provision is the second most fundamental need after relationship: New Testament scholar Simon Kistemaker wrote, "As Jesus' undershepherds, they [elders] guide his sheep to the green pastures of his Word and feed them spiritual food."[1] As a faithful coach, we provide "nourishment" to those in our care.

Timothy Laniak, speaking of his experience in caring for sheep, wrote the following:

> One thing I learned during my experience out on the range was that if you care for sheep, you feed them all the time. I was surprised when we moved three or four times throughout the day to make sure the flocks got the right mix and variety. The obvious concern was providing the flocks with adequate, balanced nutrition. When we came in at dusk, their grazing intake was supplemented again, this time with a meal of enriched grain. Feeding

is the only way to secure healthy production. Without it, there is less milk and fiber, and fewer healthy births.[2]

Jesus exhorted Peter to "feed my sheep" as a proof of his love for Jesus (John 21:17). A gospel coach will seek to feed the disciple with spiritual nourishment that will enable them to grow, flourish, and reproduce healthy spiritual offspring as an expression of love for Jesus and to the glory of God. The prophet Ezekiel emphasizes this responsibility of a shepherd when he describes God as a faithful shepherd of his own flock, his people:

> I will feed them with good pasture, and on the mountain heights of Israel shall be their grazing land. There they shall lie down in good grazing land, and on rich pasture they shall feed on the mountains of Israel. I myself will be the shepherd of my sheep, and I myself will make them lie down, declares the Lord God.
> —Ezekiel 34:14–15

The Word of God is spiritual food (Matthew 4:4). Pragmatic morsels are not the banquet food from the Lord, our shepherd-host (Psalm 23). In the words of John Calvin, sheep "cannot be fed except with pure doctrine which alone is our spiritual food."[3] We also receive spiritual nourishment directly from Jesus as well. Jesus said this about himself:

> "I am the living bread that came down from heaven. If anyone eats of this bread, he will live forever. And the bread that I will give for the life of the world is my flesh."
> The Jews then disputed among themselves, saying, "How can this man give us his flesh to eat?" So Jesus said to them, "Truly, truly, I say to you, unless you eat the flesh of the Son of Man and drink his blood, you have no life in you."
> —John 6:51–53

Ideally, a coach will design a specific diet for the exact needs of the disciple. Some disciples will need to feed on basic, foundational information (what the apostle Paul refers to as "milk" as opposed to "meat"). Other disciples may need to focus more heavily in one area of their life as opposed to the other. For example, a disciple who has been a member of a Christian community most of their life and has had very little exposure to unsaved people may need to be fed and trained in evangelism and a missional lifestyle. A gospel coach will need to appropriately apply the Word of God to their specific need and encourage them with truth, recognizing where they have aligned their life with the gospel and where they have not. A coach must be willing to humbly address the weaknesses of their disciple, rebuking their sins and strengthening their "drooping hands ... and weak knees" (Hebrews 12:12).

FEEDING QUALITIES: NOURISHING, INSPIRING, EQUIPPING

A coach provides counsel, admonishment, and encouragement for challenges. The coach speaks truth into the life of the disciple. They probe issues regarding subtle idolatries such as church, work, success, or approval. They relentlessly proclaim the truth of the gospel and its application into the life of the disciple, appropriately rebuking, reproving, and confronting the disciple to prompt them to align their living with God's truth. By declaring the truth, the coach feeds the disciple with meat and milk of the Word to develop a diet that will produce a healthy leader.

The coach relies on the Holy Spirit for the right words and tone at the right time and is utterly dependent on him to provide discernment to edify and equip. They also impart great assurance in not simply the disciple's gifts, abilities, plans, and obedience but in the Lord's promises as well. They see current realities and issues but also envision and communicate the bright hope of God's call in the disciple's life. They remind the disciple of their missional objectives, strategies, and whole-life stewardship. They bring God and his glory and promises back into the big picture, continuously reminding the disciple-leader of the life-giving gospel.

There are three key "feeding" qualities of a gospel coach: nourishing, inspiring, and equipping.

FEED AS A SHEPHERD BY NOURISHING WITH TRUTH

Leading and feeding with truth go hand in hand. A good shepherd knows what the sheep need to be healthy. They don't just feed them information; they feed them transformational bread that provides health and life. Our leading and feeding are expressions of our love for Jesus and his love for the sheep.

> When they had finished breakfast, Jesus said to Simon Peter, "Simon, son of John, do you love me more than these?" He said to him, "Yes, Lord; you know that I love you." He said to him, *"Feed my lambs."* He said to him a second time, "Simon, son of John, do you love me?" He said to him, "Yes, Lord; you know that I love you." He said to him, *"Tend [poimainō] my sheep."* He said to him the third time, "Simon, son of John, do you love me?" Peter was grieved because he said to him the third time, "Do you love me?" and he said to him, "Lord, you know everything; you know that I love you." Jesus said to him, *"Feed my sheep."*
>
> —John 21:15–17, emphasis added

Gospel coaches communicate boldly to the disciple-leaders who God is through their words and handling of Scripture (see Hebrews 1:1; John 1). The coach passionately yearns for the disciple to see God for all he is. A coach could walk a disciple through Galatians and show them the beauty of Christ's salvation accomplished for them, apart from anything they can contribute. The coach may point out how God has shown himself as loving in the disciple's life in the midst of painful circumstances. The coach's tone here is impassioned, energetic, and courageous.

FEED AS A SHEPHERD BY INSPIRING TOWARD JESUS

David is described in the book of Ezekiel as the prince leading them to the King. The role of the shepherd leader is to always point to the chief Shepherd, Jesus. He is the ultimate aim in our coaching and leading. If we seek to lead others to a ministry, a philosophy, or style, we are not shepherds but wolves (Acts 20:28). God entrusts the shepherd to lead the flock to the King, not to the prince. Our leadership must always point people to Jesus, not to ourselves: "And I will set up over them one shepherd, my servant David, and he shall feed them: he shall feed them and be their shepherd. And I, the LORD, will be their God, and my servant David shall be prince among them. I am the LORD; I have spoken" (Ezekiel 34:23–24).

A coach patiently encourages the disciple in truth, refreshes the weary disciple's soul with God's promises (Isaiah 50:4), and illuminates areas of darkness or confusion with vision (John 1; 8:31–32). In a coaching relationship, this looks like a coach responding to a disciple's frustration and despair with a reminder that God will finish the work he has started and that Jesus has paid the price in full. The coach reviews the ways God has shown the disciple that he is at work in the disciple's life. The coach displays strength, firmness, and passion in his admonition to the disciple.

A coach can inspire the person they are coaching with their own walk with God and dependence on the Holy Spirit. The coach looks to the Holy Spirit as teacher, guide, sanctifier, and affirmer of our sonship and standing before God. The Spirit is our helper in prayer and the one who directs us and empowers our witness to a lost world. The coach inspires their disciple by displaying the grace of God working in their own heart and continually sanctifying him for work they are not qualified to do or words they are not capable of fulfilling. We are all dependent on the gospel all of the time for all areas of our life.

FEED AS A SHEPHERD BY EQUIPPING PEOPLE IN THEIR NEEDS

In shepherding others, we lead them toward rest, refreshment, restoration, and repentance through the chief Shepherd, Jesus. The chief Shepherd Jesus provides all that we need, and, "I shall not want."

> The LORD is my shepherd; I shall not want.
>> He makes me lie down in green pastures.
> He leads me beside still waters.
>> He restores my soul.
> He leads me in paths of righteousness
>> for his name's sake.
>
> —Psalm 23:1–3

Practically, a gospel coach helps others find the resources, personnel, funds, information, and ideas needed to faithfully pursue the calling of God. They share their own knowledge and skills with the disciple (1 Corinthians 4:16; Philippians 3:17) and show them how the gospel applies to their need. They have experiential, detailed, and specific wisdom to offer the disciple when they are most hungry for it (1 Corinthians 11:1; Colossians 1:15–18). The equipping aspect of a relationship is exemplified in the stories of Barnabas and Paul, of Paul and Timothy, and of Paul and Titus. In our Western world, we expect to learn skills by reading about them and taking a written test. In the Eastern world (the context of the Bible), skills were imparted from one person to the other. It was life-on-life equipping. In the context of coaching, this could mean that the coach shares what worked or didn't work, for example, in their first years of church planting and then helps the disciple to consider all the needed resources. It could also be that the coach imparts the characteristics necessary to cope with impatient people. The disciple may ask the coach, "How did you do X?" and the coach will walk the disciple through the truths and experience to impart those needed skills and abilities.

Coaching systems based on the nondirective approach do not require the coach to be competent in missional skill areas since that approach is primarily about asking good questions and then allowing a person to come up with their own solutions. Coaching within our paradigm is more effective if the coach has some experience in the area of the disciple's primary ministry responsibility. It benefits the disciple for the coach to have had experienced, to some degree, what the disciple is experiencing rather than just being a sounding board or personal mirror.

In one case, a community group leader faced unfounded accusations leveled by a family in his small group. He sought coaching on how to deal with this from a fellow participant in the group. This group member suggested asking another community group leader how to deal with this delicate matter, and it was exactly what was needed. This other leader had faced a similar problem and was able to coach him by equipping him with proven principles illustrated in his own experience. There is greater credibility when someone has gone through the hardship or common challenges of a ministry skill.

A coach observes and evaluates the disciple's strength and weaknesses and then assists the disciple to establish objectives and strategies to develop the abilities and skills necessary to accomplish it. The coach teaches by providing positive and negative feedback to help the disciple to be more fruitful. Paul Stanley and Robert Clinton emphasize the importance of coaches' knowledge of their subject:

> Coaches usually know the subject they deal with inside and out. They have an overall grasp. They can break good performance down into basic skills that must be learned. They can assess the mentee's motivation and skill level and adapt appropriately. Most importantly, good coaches know how to encourage and strengthen mentees to do what is necessary to develop the skills and attitudes that will lead to excellence.[4]

Decisions made in coaching relationships have to be the result of deep saturation in gospel truth and not just relying on ideas from the corporate world or 140-character Twitter counsel. Practically, a gospel coach points their disciple to Bible passages, books, articles, blogs, media, sermons, and resources from which they can draw nourishment for their personal, spiritual, or missional lives and then be ready to be led to passionately follow God's call on their life.

CHAPTER 9

COACHING QUALITIES: LEADING

LEAD THE SHEEP

Lead: Provide direction and discernment.

Leading the flock is a key responsibility of the shepherd. David, writing of the Lord as his shepherd, states, "He *leads* me beside still waters. He restores my soul. He *leads* me in paths of righteousness for his name's sake" (Psalm 23:2–3, emphasis added). Shepherds typically lead by walking in front of the flock with an occasional look behind them, utilizing a whistle or special call to keep the flock in line. A skillful shepherd will vary their preferred leadership style to ensure that their flock is healthy and secure. Sometimes they will need to lead with tenderness and bring a flock to a place of rest and refreshment, while at other times they can lead straightforwardly with clear guidance. A shepherd may be able to lead by influence, but there will also be times when a shepherd needs to push from behind to avoid distractions and trouble. And then there are times when a shepherd can simply guide by walking alongside their disciple.

The shepherd David led Israel as faithfully as he did his flock. "With upright heart he shepherded them and guided them with his skillful hand" (Psalm 78:72). David didn't just wait for his flock to decide where to go; he led them and guided them. He led them as a follower of the good shepherd—as a sheep himself—and he led them with developed skills, competencies, wisdom, and abilities.

Jesus, the good shepherd, led his disciples as they followed his voice and were given eternal life (John 10:27–28). Faithful shepherds are simultaneously dependent sheep that lead by providing an example of following Jesus. The apostle Peter wrote about walking alongside a disciple and being "examples to the flock" (1 Peter 5:3). Likewise, the apostle Paul urged his disciples to "be imitators of me, as I am of Christ" (1 Corinthians 11:1). Paul recognized that he was both a sheep and a shepherd who imitates Jesus Christ—the good shepherd.

A gospel coach is motivated by the well-being of the disciple and is not motivated by personal gain, recognition, or credit. Timothy Witmer tells of a group of tourists in Israel who were interested in learning about shepherding after observing a shepherd with his flock of sheep. The Israeli tour guide informed the group that shepherds *always* lead their flocks from the front—they never "drive" the sheep from behind. A short time later, the group drove past a flock along the road and saw a man walking behind the flock of sheep, urging them forward. The tourists quickly called this to the guide's attention. Surprised, the tour guide stopped the bus to discuss what they had seen with the "shepherd." Boarding the bus with a sly grin on his face, he announced to his eager listeners, "That wasn't the shepherd; that was the butcher!"[1]

LEADING THROUGH CHANGE

Leading others through change is an important facet of being a gospel coach. Peacemaker Ministries has outlined a theology of change in their resource *The Leadership Opportunity* that serves as a useful guide for understanding change from a biblical perspective.

1. *God clearly prescribes personal change* (Romans 12:1). Change is God's idea. Scripture calls us to "be transformed." Scripture makes

it clear that Christians are to expect and pursue change in their personal lives. We are sanctified into the image of Christ, and that takes a lifetime of personal change. Because we all tend to walk in the same ruts, it is helpful for people to be reminded of this principle. The fact that the Christian life isn't static is not only an important concept to remember as we cooperate with God in our own sanctification; it also begins to break up the hard soil of resistance to change in the church.

2. *God clearly prescribes change in the community of his people* (Psalm 23; Ecclesiastes 3:1–8). God does not locate his people in one place and setting. God's people are constantly on the move. In Psalm 23, the shepherd leads through changing landscapes. In Ecclesiastes 3:1–8, seasons change. People must not only adapt to change but also expect change in the life of their Christian community. Nothing ultimately continues unchanged.

3. *Not all change is necessary and/or wise* (1 Corinthians 10:31; James 4:1–3). Not all of the opportunities we encounter require a change. Not all change is progress. We must first consider our own hearts. Is this God's idea, or is my own heart running the show (see James 4:1–3)? Has change and newness become my idol? We must also count the cost. It is not wise to pursue changes that yield a small benefit if they are disruptive or harmful. Pursuing difficult change that serves little outcome is madness. We don't back off from change just because the road looks tough or there is sinful resistance. But we balance the value of the change with its cost.

4. *There are many areas of church practice where God is not prescriptive.* God does not give us the final prescriptive word on style, method, and best practices. While Scripture is very clear on core doctrine and on some areas of practice, many (if not most) aspects of church life fall into the realm of wisdom and preference. When we are dealing with an area of wisdom and preference, everyone needs to take a step back. We have choices, and no one is necessarily "right" or "wrong." When an issue has to do with potential doctrinal changes, a leadership team will likely be more assertive. But where the issue is one of wisdom or preference, leaders can and should be less forceful. We must not be prescriptive where God is not. We must avoid elevating a preference to the level of absolute truth.

5. *God ordained a diverse church, and we will differ in preference.* Scripture celebrates unity, but never uniformity. We are one body with many different parts (1 Corinthians 12), and this diversity is a great strength. Diversity by its very definition means that we will view things differently—inevitably there will be disagreements and misunderstandings when change rolls around. This isn't a problem; it is healthy! Differences are a natural and healthy by-product of the diversity that God has built into the church. The wise leader will tell people there will be disagreements in preference, precisely because of the gift of diversity. If people expect differences, they are likely to react more graciously when they arise.

6. *We should recognize that it is appropriate to resist change because God has wired us to value familiarity.* Familiarity provides structure to our world. When change comes, even the godliest people experience anxiety over the unknown. It is also hard to let go of those things we treasure. It's natural, and not necessarily sinful, to want things to stay just as they are. We need to wisely and gently help people to work through the pain and uncertainty of transition. This isn't a sin or discipline issue unless accompanied by a total failure to trust God. Sometimes it's the shepherd's role to be among the worried sheep, reminding them that the Christian life entails constant change.

7. *Though resisting change is not necessarily sinful, people may also inappropriately resist change because we are naturally idolaters.* Our hearts are idol factories, and sometimes our desires escalate into sinful demands or idol making (see James 4:1–3). We stop worrying about obeying, submitting to, and honoring God and begin worrying about winning, being right, and getting our way. Gospel coaches gently bring correction and help people who are caught in idolatry. Helping our disciples get to the heart issue is critical. "If anyone is caught in any transgression, you who are spiritual should restore him in a spirit of gentleness" (Galatians 6:1). If someone is being driven by an idolatrous craving, our job as leaders is to help them see the sin in their heart and to gently but firmly lead them to repentance. When there's idolatry on both sides (idols of the old way versus idols of the new way), the lines of battle are truly drawn. At worst, this can split the church. This is a critical moment for wise but firm pastoral intervention.

8. *God clearly calls his leaders to lead gently, wisely, lovingly, and, where necessary, firmly.* The dominant biblical picture of leadership is that of a shepherd, and it is during difficult times of change that the shepherd's heart will be most evident. Change must be handled sensitively. It's all too easy when leading through change to become aggressive, force the change, and exert inappropriate pressure on the people resisting—all signs of a controlling leader. It is just as possible to avoid making needed changes by not dealing with conflict and letting it run to its conclusion. This is a sign of a people-pleasing leader. The leader who fails to act leaves some people divided and others with a sense of aimlessness and frustration. Gently leading and loving their people through difficult times are key responsibilities of wise shepherds.

9. *God clearly calls his people to respectfully follow their leaders.* Believers are called to follow leaders in a certain way. Hebrews 13:17 reads, "Obey your leaders ..." God calls us to honor and respect the leaders he has placed over us, with a spirit of joy and not groaning (not being a burden), even when decisions don't go our way. Leaders' decisions are certain to be unpopular with some people some of the time. At those moments, the congregation's response is very important. Genuine concerns are fine, and questions should be aired respectfully and appropriately. However, gossip, slander, undermining accusations, and faction-forming criticisms are sinful, unbiblical, and inappropriate patterns of behavior. In times of change, remind people of their calling as followers. People need to maintain an appropriate biblical perspective on the authority and responsibility of their leaders to lead them. Beware of a "marketing" mind-set in which people start to think of themselves as customers and thus that the church exists only to please them. When this happens, the church becomes completely driven by members' whims and preferences. Churches that treat their people like customers don't tend to talk much about sin, repentance, or the need for a Savior.

10. *We must always remember that it is the gospel that enables change.* As I ponder God's laying down his right to punish me (and instead punishing Christ in my place), I am set free to lay down my "rights" to get what I want. In Matthew 18, in the parable of the unmerciful

servant, Jesus clearly teaches that the one who has received much mercy can and should be willing to lay down their rights to what they want or are entitled to. That person should consistently point people to the gospel. When we really understand how God forgives us and who we are in Christ, we are willing to lay down our preferences. The more we soak in the gospel, the easier change becomes.[2]

LEADING QUALITIES: INVESTING, OVERSEEING, GUIDING

The third role of a coach is to shepherd by *leading the sheep*. A coach provides investment, oversight, and guidance for decisions. The Scriptures plainly declare "the LORD has established his throne in the heavens, and his kingdom rules over all" (Psalm 103:19). He is Lord over his creation and rules as a shepherd. A coach evaluates the needs of the disciple, observes them in action, and imparts skills as needed. The coach is not simply solving or fixing problems but is working to lead the disciple to accomplish what God has impassioned them to do.

The coach who leads others is hardworking, disciplined, and generous. A coach helps a disciple to look at problems and find solutions. They have to be willing to enter chaos to help the disciple to organize their life from the grandest scale to the smallest detail for the enjoyment and benefit of the disciple. To coach as a shepherd, a person may need to make personal sacrifices for the good of those being coached.

The coach is often able to be a resource, connecting their disciple-leader with others, such as fellow church leaders and subject matter experts who can help them with such specific areas of need—legal issues, facility searches, relocation needs, or specialized ministries. The coach in this way acts more like a concierge and less like an expert or a resource.

There are three key "leading" qualities of a gospel coach: investing, overseeing, and guiding.

LEAD AS A SHEPHERD BY INVESTING SACRIFICIALLY

As God entrusts people to us, we are to humbly image his care for them through our sacrificial leadership in their lives. A shepherd endures hardship for the good of the sheep, especially when to do so may be uncomfortable and dangerous. Jesus guarded the gate with his own life — sacrificially.

> So Jesus again said to them, "Truly, truly, I say to you, I am the door of the sheep. All who came before me are thieves and robbers, but the sheep did not listen to them. I am the door. If anyone enters by me, he will be saved and will go in and out and find pasture. The thief comes only to steal and kill and destroy. I came that they may have life and have it abundantly. I am the good shepherd. The good shepherd lays down his life for the sheep. He who is a hired hand and not a shepherd, who does not own the sheep, sees the wolf coming and leaves the sheep and flees, and the wolf snatches them and scatters them. He flees because he is a hired hand and cares nothing for the sheep"
> —John 10:7–13

In perhaps one of his greatest paradoxes, Jesus continually states that true greatness and authority are marked by self-sacrificing behavior (Matthew 20:26–28). The coach willingly gives their time and energy to produce a healthy, reproducing disciple (1 Peter 5:2–3). They invest into the disciple by training in skills, character, and leading others (2 Timothy 4:16–17). They joyfully share resources, generously gifting and equipping the disciple to accomplish their passion for God (Ephesians 4:11–12). A coach may offer good books or connections with helpful people and perhaps even provide ideas for needed education. The coach stands with nothing to gain from the relationship but generously invests in the disciple.

LEAD AS A SHEPHERD BY OVERSEEING EVERY ASPECT OF A PERSON'S LIFE

We lead effectively by willingly exercising oversight for the other person's good personally, spiritually, and missionally. A good shepherd is not motivated for personal gain.

> So I exhort the elders among you, as a fellow elder and a witness of the sufferings of Christ, as well as a partaker in the glory that is going to be revealed: shepherd the flock of God that is among

you, *exercising oversight*, not under compulsion, but willingly, as God would have you; not for shameful gain, but eagerly; not domineering over those in your charge, but being examples to the flock. And when the chief Shepherd appears, you will receive the unfading crown of glory.

—1 Peter 5:1–4, emphasis added

Sheep scatter without a shepherd. They run when they sense danger. An effective coach cares about a person's whole life, not just isolated aspects of it. A leader must spend time among the flock to accomplish this and be willing to take courageous initiative without abuse. A coach asks difficult questions for the good of the disciple and the glory of a caring Redeemer. The careful and meticulous oversight of a flock by a shepherd is necessary to lead them beside still waters and toward green pastures. The coach exemplifies for the disciple a life that practices redemptive, dominion-like ministry in the manner of Jesus (Hebrews 2:8; Revelation 21). They are sober-minded, self-controlled, and disciplined and have a well-managed household (1 Timothy 3:3; Titus 1:5–9). They know how to manage themselves and those closest to them, but they rely on the grace and power of God for this rather than overpowering those under them (1 Peter 5:2–3). They are actively pursuing a redeemed life where righteousness and peace rule down to every last detail (John 14:3; Revelation 21). The disciple is able to see "what it really looks like" to live in joy and in obedience to Jesus when they observe the life of their coach.

LEAD AS A SHEPHERD BY GUIDING WITH SPIRIT-EMPOWERED DISCERNMENT

A leader discerns truth and helps to dispel the lies of Satan that we are all prone to believe. This requires Spirit empowered discernment: "When the Spirit of truth comes, he will guide you into all the truth, for he will not speak on his own authority, but whatever he hears he will speak, and he will declare to you the things that are to come. He will glorify me, for he will take what is mine and declare it to you" (John 16:13–14).

A gospel coach helps the disciple-leader to choose the best path for their life. It requires an upright heart and skill (Proverbs 15:22; 24:6).

They stir the confidence of the disciple to trust Jesus' grace and redemption in their life (Hebrews 4:16; 10:19–23). They do this through extending grace when the disciple fails. They model forgiveness and pray for and with the disciple (Hebrews 5:7) and treat the disciple as one who is righteous with a clean conscience in light of the truth (Hebrews 9:11–14). Above all, they are ceaselessly inviting the Holy Spirit's work, presence, and power into the life of the disciple as the ongoing support available to all believers (Hebrews 9:8). They use discernment and wisdom to help the disciple to sort through choices, make decisions, and develop strategies in every aspect of their life.

CHAPTER 10

COACHING QUALITIES: PROTECTING

PROTECT THE SHEEP

> Protect: Provide defense against sinful behaviors
> (prone to wander) and errant doctrine
> (false prophets in sheep's clothing).

In Istanbul, Turkey, a stunned Turkish shepherd watched as one lone sheep jumped from a cliff to its death. Then, before he realized what was happening, he watched as nearly 1,500 other sheep followed, each leaping off the same cliff. By the time he was able to stop the flock from leaping over the edge, nearly 450 dead animals lay on top of one another in a billowy white pile. Thankfully, many of the 1,500 who jumped were spared death as their fall was cushioned by the growing height of the pile of dead animals.[1]

Shepherds are watchmen who keep guard over their flock. Our good shepherd, who laid down his life for his sheep (John 10:11), is the only lasting and true source of unshakable safety and shelter. The psalmist assures us, "Even though I walk through the valley of the shadow of death, I will fear no evil, for you are with me; your rod and your staff, they comfort me" (Psalm 23:4). The good shepherd provides protection from the gravest danger of all—judgment for our sins.

A coach pays careful attention to those they are coaching. They oversee their life and warn them against being misled by other leaders. They defend against spiritual attack by the Enemy. The coach does this with unceasing courage and compassion (Acts 20:28). Sheep wander into danger, and a selfish shepherd will flee when danger arises. But a faithful shepherd lays down their life to protect the sheep. They protect the sheep by being on the alert at all times (Acts 20:31).

There are at least five distinct ways in which a gospel coach protects their disciple-leader:

1. *Protect with compassion (love).* Jesus "had compassion for them, because they were harassed and helpless, like sheep without a shepherd" (Matthew 9:36). Love for Jesus and love for his sheep are essential to effectively shepherding another person. Without this characteristic, the relationship will be clinical and professional and will lack gospel transformation. We cannot effectively protect those we do not love.

2. *Protect with courage (faith).* The coach pursues the disciple in their rebellion, apathy, or sin and holds them accountable for purity of life and doctrine. We must have the courage to confront others in love as a regular pattern of our relationship. We must be willing to enact discipline in response to their actions when necessary (Matthew 18:15–17). They need us and want us to regularly monitor the fences in their life.

3. *Protect by contact (community).* A shepherd is an overseer watching for deviancy and a disciple's tendency to escape or wander away in isolation. Jesus told the parable of a man with a hundred sheep, one of which went astray. He suggested that a good shepherd would leave the ninety-nine and search for the one that wandered from the fold (Mat-

thew 18:12–13). When they are in community with the disciple, the coach will recognize a wandering disciple.

4. *Protect with calling (passion).* The local church confirms the calling to oversee specific disciples (Acts 13:1–3; 20:28). Coaches must examine their hearts, their motivation, and the cost to their lives as they follow this calling.

5. *Protect with commitment (generosity).* Shepherding others requires a generous commitment of time, relational energy, and focus. We can't coach others halfheartedly. God rebuked this lack of commitment: "The weak you have not strengthened, the sick you have not healed, the injured you have not bound up, the strayed you have not brought back, the lost you have not sought, and with force and harshness you have ruled them. So they were scattered, because there was no shepherd" (Ezekiel 34:4–5).

PROTECTING QUALITIES: DISPLAYING COMPASSION, COMFORTING, FIGHTING

The role of protecting a disciple is a function of a gospel-centered coach who has a ministry of caring for, confronting, and walking alongside the disciple through the rough terrain of life. The protecting coach counsels and listens well, with the goal of ministering God's protection and presence. A gospel-centered coach functions in a protective role. They acknowledge that the disciple is wrestling daily with doubt, fear, pride, and idolatry. They understand the natural propensity of the disciple-leader to relate to other people, their own work, and their own marriage and to respond in ways that might serve their own desire for power, approval, comfort, and security. The coach as protector diagnoses possible subtle ways that sin is invading the disciple's heart and affecting their approach to life. The coach will remind the disciple of God's love, Spirit empowerment, and sovereign reign in their life.

Sheep are completely defenseless in their natural environment. They are not fierce defenders of their domains. They are furry and cute and have limited senses. Their only defense is to flock together with other sheep. A lone sheep will surely be killed without the protective (and constant) oversight of the shepherd or the security of the flock. After a tragic ending to the careers of two church-planting pastors who operated outside of the oversight of other shepherds, Acts 29 Network enacted a "no rogue planters" mandate among its nearly five hundred members. We identified five planters who were not interacting with others in the network and confronted them. Two of them repented and gathered inside the protection of the network once again. One resigned, and two others were pursued further, without much immediate response. Within thirty days of confronting these men, both fell into sexual immorality with members of their church. It was later discovered that they had engaged in this activity for several years with multiple partners. Though it is not entirely clear if they were on their own because they were involved in this sin or if they fell into sin because they were on their own, much of the evidence suggests the latter. A gospel coach takes this role of protecting others seriously.

There are three key "protecting" qualities of a gospel coach: displaying compassion, comforting, and fighting.

PROTECTING AS A SHEPHERD BY DISPLAYING COMPASSION

Compassionate love is the basis of leadership. A leader's primary love is for Jesus and not just for others. If the primary love is for those we are leading, then we attempt to please them and will likely be disappointed. A gospel coach is an undershepherd of Jesus. A leader loves the sheep compassionately because Jesus loves the sheep. Jesus' compassion for the helpless and harassed sheep resulted in a call for more leaders: "When [Jesus] saw the crowds, he had compassion for them, because they were harassed and helpless, like sheep without a shepherd. Then he said to his disciples, 'The harvest is plentiful, but the laborers are few; therefore pray earnestly to the Lord of the harvest to send out laborers into his harvest'" (Matthew 9:37–38).

A leader's care is merciful, sympathetic (Hebrews 3:17), and gentle, for they are aware of their own flaws (Hebrews 5:5). This care enables the disciple to humble themselves before God and their coach and receive counsel. Christ's care for us, as illustrated in 1 Peter 5:6–7, is the motivation to humble ourselves before him and entrust our lives to him. We can show this care to our disciple through the development of listening skills. Most of what we hear we forget or misinterpret because we have not learned to listen. We need to hear with our minds but also with our hearts and with our souls and with all our strength. We need to be motivated by the gospel and not just by ministering to the other person.

Four principles of listening emerge from the gospel.

1. The gospel reminds us that listening is an *act of grace* extended to the other person. In the same way that we do not deserve an audience with God, neither does a disciple-leader necessarily deserve an audience with us.

2. We are reminded that listening is an *act of love*. We display God's unmerited love to us when we listen to others with the motivation to care for them.

3. The gospel helps us to remember that listening is an *act of compassion*. When we listen to another person, we are displaying empathy and sympathy for the issues, challenges, and celebrations they are experiencing. My brother took his own life in 2011. I went to dinner in New York City with John and Shari Thomas, leaders at Redeemer Presbyterian in Manhattan. Shari asked me about my brother's death and the effect it had on me. I gave a standard answer, not wanting to burden them about the pain I was experiencing. In spite of that, Shari compassionately asked me more. I found myself talking freely, and Shari listened with such a pronounced compassion that while I was speaking, I had a fresh awareness of God's compassion for me in my pain.

4. The gospel teaches us that listening is an *act of participation with the Holy Spirit*. We must listen responsively to the Spirit, who may want to reveal Scriptures and their applications that we may never come up with through our own wisdom.

Dietrich Bonheoffer once wrote the following:

The first service that one owes to others in the fellowship consists in listening to them. Just as love to God begins with listening to his Word, so the beginning of love for the brethren is learning to listen to them. It is God's love for us that he not only gives us his Word but also lends us his ear. So it is his work that we do for our brother when we learn to listen to him.[2]

PROTECT AS A SHEPHERD BY COMFORTING WITH HOPE IN THE GOSPEL

Revelation 7:15–17 points us to the fulfillment of Psalm 23:

Therefore they are before the throne of God,
    and serve him day and night in his temple;
and he who sits on the throne will shelter them with his presence.
They shall hunger no more, neither thirst anymore;
    the sun shall not strike them,
    nor any scorching heat.
For the Lamb in the midst of the throne will be their shepherd,
    and he will guide them to springs of living water,
and God will wipe away every tear from their eyes.
                                                    —Revelation 7:15–17

We are suffering now, but one day we will have our hope realized through the Lamb of God—our Shepherd-King Jesus—when every form of suffering will be removed. Our calling is not to teach people to cope with their pains but rather to lead them to the streams of living water that our Lord Shepherd provides. Our hope does not reside here ultimately. The coach protects others through their discouragement and in their anger by reminding them of their hope of eternal life. Life is sometimes temporarily painful, but Jesus is always eternally glorious.

When a coach has pointed out an error or has uncovered seemingly insurmountable tasks, a protecting coach will walk alongside a disciple through conviction, repentance, surrender, pleading, and need. Rather than avoiding the ugly mess of sin, a coach courageously walks alongside their disciple, pointing them to Christ for all their healing and redemption (Hebrews 9:11–14). They do not leave the disciple to figure it out and clean themselves up, but they reassure them of their presence in this situation. This is not codependence, but rather godly interdependence as the coach functions through the mercy of Jesus in the life of the disciple, building them up in love (Ephesians 4:16). This may mean changing an entire coaching session at the last minute to deal with pain and suffering in the life of the disciple, calling them more frequently through a dark season, joining them for a difficult conversation, or assisting in the completion of some specific tasks that they cannot finish on their own.

PROTECT AS A SHEPHERD BY FIGHTING FOR THE GOOD OF OTHERS

We don't tolerate wolves; we fight them. You can identify a wolf when leaders attempt to draw disciples to themselves rather than to the chief Shepherd Jesus. If a shepherd loves the flock, they will fight for their safety. If a church leader is afraid to fight wolves, the flock will be in constant danger. The authority to fight comes from God. Our enemy is real, and therefore an unceasing commitment is needed.

> Pay careful attention to yourselves and to all the flock, in which the Holy Spirit has made you overseers, to care for the church of God, which he obtained with his own blood. I know that after my departure fierce wolves will come in among you, not sparing the flock; and from among your own selves will arise men speaking twisted things, to draw away the disciples after them. Therefore be alert, remembering that for three years I did not cease night or day to admonish everyone with tears.
>
> —Acts 20:28–31

As shepherd-leaders, we are to be on guard—for ourselves and for the flock because the Holy Spirit has appointed us to oversee a flock that was obtained by the shed blood of Jesus, and because they are threatened by wolves and by thieves. Shepherd leaders are able to do this by working day and night to warn the flock regularly and compassionately with the Word of God. Our confidence is not in ourselves but in the Word of God that is able to bring health and maturity to the flock.

The coach confronts the disciple with truth, pointing out their error and where their life does not match the gospel (Galatians 2:11; Titus 1:9; Hebrews 2:2–3). The coach fights for the good of the disciple to protect them from sin and self-deception, and may do so by reproving, rebuking, and exhorting them (2 Timothy 4:2). The protecting coach is not swayed from their own commitment to truth by fearing what the disciple or anyone else will think of them (Isaiah 50:6–7; Luke 4:23–30). They are restless until they see the disciple living in the gospel's freedom and righteousness. They fight for the good of the disciple with words of encouragement.

Affirmation—not empty praise—is a gospel exercise of pointing out where a person lives in line with the gospel and how they are demonstrating the fruit of the Spirit in their lives. Hebrews 10:24 encourages this, exhorting us to "consider how to stir up one another to love and good works." Sam Crabtree gives us four helpful characteristics of affirmation. He emphasizes that effective affirmations are *detached from correction* (not sandwiched between criticisms). They have an *ongoing steady flow* and are not something that is rarely shared. Good affirmation is rooted in *honest, commendable traits*, not exaggerations. And finally, it ultimately centers on the *work of God in a person's life*, not simply emphasizing external traits or abilities.[3]

Church leadership is shepherding. In 2 Timothy, we see Paul coaching Timothy in the four realms of shepherding.

1. Paul *knew* Timothy. He referred to Timothy as his "beloved son," and he mentioned the faith of his mother and grandmother (1:2, 5). He had a meaningful relationship with Timothy and was aware of his weaknesses.
2. Paul *fed* Timothy with sound words and entrusted him with the gospel (1:13–14).
3. Paul *led* Timothy to entrust the gospel to faithful men who could train others as well (2:2).
4. Paul *protected* Timothy. Paul spent most of his time in this second letter to Timothy expressing his desire to protect him. He prayed for him constantly (1:3) and communicated a longing to spend time with Timothy, even though Timothy was struggling (1:4). He encouraged him in his growing faith and urged him to fight against fear (1:5–7). He protected Timothy by reminding him of the hope of the gospel and the shared suffering we all experience as followers of Christ and proclaimers of this gospel (1:8–14).

PART 3

COACHING SESSIONS

CHAPTER 11

A GOSPEL COACHING CONVERSATION

WHAT IS GOSPEL COACHING? At its core, it is a conversation informed and guided by the truth of the gospel message. While it includes asking good questions, it also involves give-and-take, advice and direction, inquiry and consideration. Since it is a conversation, it means that the coach will listen, observe, respond, interact, offer insights, support, encourage, and sometimes give directions. Good coaches are good conversationalists. When you coach a leader, you spend much of your time together trying to ask them good questions — probing questions, hard questions — but you will also be answering many questions. This is what a good, healthy relationship looks like. To coach other leaders, you must be able to share stories of success *and* failure in order to give the leader wisdom and ways of applying the truth.

There are many contributing factors to an effective coaching session. Ultimately it is the Holy Spirit's work that makes any session successful or effects any change and growth in the heart of the disciple. However, the coach can cooperate with and serve under the Holy Spirit in practical ways that are not just mysterious or theoretical.

ASK GOOD QUESTIONS

Asking good questions is the key to knowing the disciple and to discovering what areas of growth are necessary (skills, competencies, weaknesses, needed areas of repentance). The skill of asking good questions will enable the coach to identify areas in which to probe further. I have developed a list of questions to help coaches in their tasks of knowing, leading, feeding, and protecting their disciples in their personal, spiritual, and missional lives. Here are a few of these questions (for the full list, see appendix 4):

Shepherding Roles	Personally	Spiritually	Missionally
Know the sheep	How did you become a Christian?	What is God doing in your heart right now?	What opportunities have you had for sharing your faith?
Feed the sheep	What is God teaching you about your role as a husband and father/wife and mother/single person?	What information or resources would be helpful for your spiritual growth?	What resources do you need to accomplish your ministry goals?
Lead the sheep	How are you personally leading others in your family?	How is the Lord leading you to respond to him?	What is the mission of your ministry?
Protect the sheep	What temptations occur in your personal life?	What priority do you give to Bible reading and prayer in your life?	Where are you prone to waste time in ministry?

Table 5: Coaching Questions for the Shepherding Roles

LISTENING IS AN ACT OF GRACE AND WISDOM

In addition to asking questions, a good coach is a good listener. Listening is not a passive formality of coaching. It is a powerful tool that allows a coach to communicate care and to see the needs of the disciple more clearly. Michael Coggin has written about the significance of listening from a biblical standpoint:

> We see in Scripture that Jesus understood the importance of listening. Even as a young boy he was sitting with the teachers in the temple, "listening to them and asking them questions and everyone was amazed at his understanding" (Luke 2:46–47). The apostle Paul understood that listening requires diligent work. When he was before Agrippa, he said, "I beg you to listen to me patiently" (Acts 26:3). The book of James tells us to "be quick to listen and slow to speak" (James 1:19). And the book of Proverbs says, "He who answers before listening—that is his folly and his shame" (Proverbs 18:13). The word *listen* occurs more than two hundred times in the Scriptures.[1]

Tips for Asking Good Questions

1. Listen longer than you think is necessary.
2. Use the comments "Tell me more ..." and "What else?" to encourage them to explore their options and their hidden motivations.
3. Ask open-ended questions primarily.
4. Ask probing questions.
5. Listen closely and summarize before asking another question. Say, "What I hear you saying is ..."

How can you practice listening in your session together? How long do you spend listening? When is it appropriate to make a judgment or give advice based on what you've heard? For those of you who are more comfortable sharing your thoughts than listening to others, this may be the most difficult aspect of your coaching relationship. For others, listening may be more instinctive, but all of us will experience trouble in directing and focusing our listening at times. I think it is safe to say that we all need to learn to listen with intentionality.

There are five key elements of active listening to help ensure that you actually hear the other person and that the other person knows you are hearing what they are saying. In many ways, this is nothing more than "Listening 101," but it still serves as a helpful reminder:

1. *Pay attention.* Give the speaker your undivided attention and acknowledge the message. Look at the person directly, maintaining eye contact. Put aside distracting thoughts. Don't mentally prepare a rebuttal. Avoid being distracted by environmental factors, including reading e-mail or browsing the Internet. "Listen" to the person's body language, tone of voice, and verbal pacing.

2. *Show that you are listening.* Use your own body language, gestures. and tone of voice to convey your attention. Note your posture—is it open and inviting? Encourage the person to continue with small verbal comments such as "yes" and "uh-huh."

3. *Provide feedback.* As a listener, your role is to understand what is being said. This may require you to reflect what is being said and ask questions. Reflect what has been said by paraphrasing. "What I'm hearing is ..." and "It sounds like you are saying ..." are great ways to reflect back. Ask questions to clarify certain points. "What do you mean when you say ...?" or "Is this what you mean?" Summarize the speaker's comments periodically.

4. *Defer judgment.* Interrupting is a waste of time. Allow the disciple an opportunity to finish. Don't interrupt with counterarguments. The coaching environment is a great place to explore new ideas—even if they are not fully developed.

5. *Respond appropriately.* Active listening is a model for respect and understanding. You are gaining information and perspective. You add nothing by attacking the speaker or otherwise putting them down. Be candid, open, and honest in your response. Assert your opinions respectfully. Shepherd the person's soul with responses and not reactions to their words, attitude, or decisions.[2]

The more time you spend listening and trying to really understand the person you are coaching, the more you will be surprised at how often your original assumptions completely miss their real heart issues. Listening to a person's answers is not to be confused with what we earlier discussed as client-centered coaching. It is a way of showing respect to the other person and a necessary step in gaining accurate understanding of their life, their heart, and their struggles. You can only appropriately direct and help the disciple by listening well.

Another element of listening that is often forgotten is allowing space for the Holy Spirit to work directly in the life of the disciple. As the disciple is verbally processing with you, the Holy Spirit may directly reveal biblical wisdom or application. If you hold too tightly to what you assume the problem is, you may conclude and push for something contrary to the Spirit's leading.

If a coach is not careful to listen to the disciple or the Holy Spirit and instead relies on their own wisdom or insight, they may end up discussing real problems that never get to the root issues to

Donna, who was coaching Anna for the first time, asked her to identify the top three challenges in her life. Anna responded by saying that working too much, her relationship with her roommate, and not getting exercise were her top concerns. Donna asked her which of these may be the most important one to focus on. After Anna thought for a moment, she responded "My relationship with my roommate."

Donna disagreed with Anna's conclusion and began trying to persuade her that the real problem was her workaholic tendency and that they should focus on that, since it was affecting both her relationship with her roommate and her time to exercise. She kept drilling Anna with questions about how her identity was found in her work. Finally, slightly exasperated, Anna blurted out, "I don't love work. I work late because I don't want to go home and face my roommate who is always mad at me!" In that moment, the Holy Spirit revealed to both of them that the real issue was not being a workaholic but rather a friendship strained by sin and bitterness. As her coach, Donna was finally able to see this and help Anna work through her resentment and hurt in her relationship with her roommate. Later, with the relationship restored, Anna's work schedule became balanced, because she now looked forward to going home at the end of the day to see her roommate.

which the truth of the gospel needs to be understood and applied. In the Acts 29 Network, our coaches have affirmed over and over again that the single most important thing they have taken away from their coaching training is the need to listen well—and to listen much longer than they initially felt was necessary.

WORKING THROUGH A GOSPEL LIFE PLAN

In addition to asking good questions and listening well, it will be helpful to spend time in your coaching sessions working through a "gospel life plan." A gospel life plan is one of the most important tools you can implement in a coaching environment. Most people have only a vague idea about what they are supposed to be doing with their life, how they're going to get there, and how to monitor progress toward accomplishing what they think they're supposed to do. As a result, they are not fully living out the calling God has for them.

Some leaders resemble too closely Alice, Lewis Carroll's fictitious character in *Alice's Adventures in Wonderland*. Alice wanders around aimlessly while inexplicable and unrelated things happen to her. When Alice bumps into the Cheshire Cat, she asks, "Would you tell me, please, which way I ought to go from here?" The cat responds, "That depends a good deal on where you want to get to."

Alice says, "I don't much care where." The cat then comments, "Then it doesn't matter which way you go." Church leaders need to clearly know where they are headed.

Below are five reasons you need to commit your goals to writing.

1. It helps articulate and clarify your calling. What are you supposed to be doing?
2. It forces you to prioritize the most important aspects of your life.
3. It motivates you toward action steps. Writing goals down and reviewing them are important so that you can follow up with action.
4. It is a formidable defense against resistance — an insidious foe to distract you from passionately pursuing your God-given calling. Written goals remind you not to quit or get distracted with "good" offers.
5. It forces you to review, reflect on, and rewrite your current goals and then return with more clarity of purpose and more fortitude to accomplish the work you believe God has called you to.

As we consider this for coaching, it suggests that church leaders can help their disciples in four specific areas:

1. understanding *how* God has called them
2. identifying *what* God has called them to do
3. deciding what *specific steps* can be taken to accomplish those goals
4. stewarding the *resources, time, and energy* that are being used to meet the goals

The graphic below (Figure 9) shows how this gospel life plan works as one unified plan in four segments. In many organizations, a mission statement will lead the company's decisions and determine the strategies they choose to pursue. But over time, a company may lose sight of their mission statement and begin to focus simply on the tasks in front of them. What they find themselves doing often has nothing to do with their original mission statement. When this occurs, an organization, a church, a school, or even a home begins

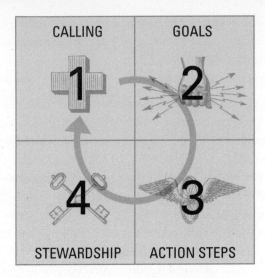

Figure 9: Gospel Life Plan

to diminish in its effectiveness. This is why we intentionally keep all four segments together in one unified plan, so the goals, actions steps, and resources used can be seen in relation to the calling—the mission that God has called this disciple to accomplish.

For a disciple-leader, the gospel life plan serves as a compass on the coaching journey. It progresses from one segment to another:

1. *Calling.* The disciple-leader discerns their calling from God, the purpose or mission that defines their service to God.
2. *Goals.* These are the high-level, big-picture goal(s) that a disciple-leader identifies that will enable them to accomplish that call.
3. *Actions Steps.* These are specific steps that a disciple-leader carries out, leading to the advancement of the goals.
4. *Stewardship.* To avoid imbalance and unhealthy patterns, the advancement of the goals through specific steps of action is governed by whole-life stewardship of time, resources, abilities, relationships, and knowledge.

The cycle then continues again, as the coach and the disciple repeatedly examine the stewardship of time, resources, abilities, relationships, and knowledge in light of the disciple's calling—whether it is the original calling or a new calling that has come to light through this process. That calling is repeatedly reviewed in light of new insight or direction and the ongoing spiritual maturity of the disciple.

CALLING

When most people hear about a "calling of God" on a person's life, they typically think about someone being called as a pastor or missionary, or perhaps as a teacher or doctor. Rarely do we think about the fact that *every* believer is called to ministry—especially if that calling differs from their occupation, from the work they do to earn a paycheck. This limiting sense of a call from God is a problem in the church today that reflects a lie the church is guilty of perpetuating. The apostle Peter clearly teaches that each and every believer has received a gift from the Lord, and he instructs believers to use the gift or gifts they have received to serve one another as good stewards of God's grace (1 Peter 4:10).

Having a "call to ministry" has long been thought of as a dramatic kind of experience, similar to what the apostle Paul had on the road to Damascus or what Martin Luther experienced as he traveled to Erfurt in 1505, where he was studying to be a lawyer. A dramatic thunderstorm terrified Luther into making a "foxhole commitment" to give up law and become a priest. The vast majority of people in the church fail to have this kind of supernatural "calling" experience.

Instead of thinking of God's call as a unique, dramatic experience, let me suggest that there are two types of call to ministry—a general calling of all believers and a specific calling for some. My initial calling began as a more general calling. I was passionately following the mission of God and serving him in the local church. Some weeks, this was taking up to thirty hours of my time as I would share Jesus with teenagers. I was also working a full-time job that consumed about forty-eight hours each week, and I found that I didn't have enough time to support myself *and* follow my passion to make disciples. My pastor recognized this and eventually hired me full-time at the church.

But I have also experienced a specific calling from God. During time spent with the Lord, I began to sense a burden and felt the Holy Spirit calling me to pastor in a specific city. I told no one of this calling. Then one day I was approached by a person who lived in that city to consider applying to serve as a pastor at a church that was in serious need of being replanted. After a formal visit, the church extended me an invitation to serve as their lead pastor, and my local church confirmed this calling. In 2003, I attended my first Acts 29 Boot Camp in Seattle just before we set out to begin this new church. After several sessions, Eric Brown, the director of Acts 29 at the time, stood to address the forty attendees. The Holy Spirit immediately impressed on my heart that he wanted me to lead the Acts 29 Network one day. I never shared this impression with anyone, including my wife. But it was a confirming sign to me when, three years later, Mark Driscoll asked me to take over Acts 29 as the director. Mark had no idea that I had felt called to the role before he unexpectedly extended the invitation to serve in that capacity. After he extended a formal offer, it wasn't a difficult decision for me to make because it was consistent with the general calling I had sensed from God—to make disciples—and it matched a specific calling of the Holy Spirit that I had sensed three years earlier—to lead Acts 29.

In both cases, there was a general calling and a specific calling. The pattern of calling is modeled in Acts 13, when the Holy Spirit was present while the believers were worshiping and fasting and said to them, "Set apart for me Barnabas and Saul for the work to which I have called them" (Acts 13:2). First, note the *inward* sense of the Holy Spirit calling, like being drafted for something. Barnabas and Saul didn't just get up, leave, and follow that call. Instead, the local church *confirmed* the call after a time of prayer and fasting, and then the church laid hands on them and sent them off. The second aspect of calling is confirmation by the church's leadership. It is common today for someone to simply announce that they were called by God in a private, subjective way. And rarely does anyone argue with them, even if they have suspicions that it may not be a genuine call. This is why confirmation by the church is essential. While a private sense of God calling may be genuine, it needs to be confirmed and supported by the local church and its leaders. This is the pattern we also see with Paul (Acts 9:26–31), Philip (Acts 8), and Barnabas (Acts 11:19–26). But there is a third aspect as well: a *context or situation* that needs addressing. In Acts 13:2, we read that Barnabas and Saul are set apart "for the work to which I have called them." In Paul's case, it was to be a church-planting missionary to the Gentiles.

While I cannot deny that pastors, missionaries, teachers, and doctors may sense a specific calling to a vocational form of ministry or work, we should not forget that sitting in the pews of churches around the world are literally millions of God-gifted, God-called believers who are his instruments for making disciples of all nations. There are mechanics, dentists, computer engineers, administrative assistants, and entrepreneurs who are passionate for the homeless, the hungry, and the addicted. While we are all called to make disciples, to glorify God, and to bear spiritual fruit, the general calling that each of us answers may look different from anyone else's calling. The truth is that 98 percent of ministers are not ordained—serving in grocery stores, as business executives, as artists and engineers—but their calling to ministry is just as valid as that of a pastor or missionary.

I know of a successful businessman who made millions of dollars before God saved him. As a new believer with a desire to follow his passion and start new churches, he considered leaving his business and becoming a church planter. His pastor wisely asked him how many churches he felt that he could personally support if he continued in corporate business and instead gave proceeds from his financial gain to help start churches. He thought about it and decided that he was not being called to become yet another poor church planter— we have lots of those—but to financially support hundreds of church planters with a percentage of his earnings. His calling *was* indeed to plant churches, but he was able to do this as a business owner, not as a pastor. Yet his calling is just as valid as that of a full-time pastor planting a church.

God calls every believer to do good works that he has uniquely prepared his children to do: "We are his workmanship, created in Christ Jesus for good works, which God prepared beforehand, that we should walk in them" (Ephesians 2:10). It is a myth to believe that God has only called people who serve in full-time vocational ministry to be missionaries. We falsely teach that the role of laity is relegated to supporting these special few who are called and chosen to do the "real" work. We have a great opportunity today to promote a renewed understanding that *each* member of the body of Christ is called to glorify God by ministering in the mission of God: "For just as the body is one and has many members, and all the members of the body, though many, are one body, so it is with Christ . . . But as it is, God arranged the members in the body, each one of them, as he chose" (1 Corinthians 12:12, 18).

Scripture teaches that God is no respecter of persons. While everyone is not equal in every way, each child of God is equally important to Father God. God has made each person unique, and God has a ministry calling for every believer. Nonvocational ministers have more to offer than just handing out bulletins and serving on committees. The job of the vocational minister is to recognize that each believer is given the manifestation of the Spirit for the common good (1 Corinthians 12:7), to help others identify their calling, and to equip the saints for the work of the ministry and for the building up of the body of Christ (Ephesians 4:11–16). We must encourage the calling of *every* believer in the church to ministry. The ability of the church to impact its culture is not limited to its pastors or vocational ministers. The more the congregation is dependent on vocational pastors, the less a nonvocational leader feels they have anything to offer. An important aspect of the coaching process is helping a person discern God's call on their life and then encourage them to passionately pursue it.

Our actions do not precede our identity; rather, it is our identity that precedes our actions. Who we are in Christ leads to what we do. When we recognize that we are God's workmanship, created in Christ Jesus, and that we are the chosen ambassadors of the King, our actions follow from that. Typically, though, we reverse this and rely on our actions—what we do—to define who we are. We tell people, "I am a doctor"; "I am a lawyer"; "I am an alcoholic." Instead of defining us by what we do, God identifies us as someone who belongs to him. C. S. Lewis has said, "The more we get what we now call 'ourselves' out of the way and let [God] take us over, the more truly ourselves we become."[3] What Lewis means is that our identity as a Christian is wrapped up in our calling by God to be his child. It is not wrapped up in our natural identity.

Most people do not know *who* God has called them to be, so they struggle to know *what* God has called them to do. As a result, they spend their lives doing what is right in front of them. Their lives are preoccupied by what is most urgent or by what others tell them to do, and they fail to accomplish what God has called them to do. Tim Keller suggests that there are three parts to discerning a call on our lives.[4] The questions focus on our passion, the people in our lives, and the places where we might pursue our calling:

1. *Passion.* What is the passion that God has placed on my heart?
2. *People.* What credible friends are urging me to follow this calling?
3. *Place.* What opportunities do I have to follow this passion or to pursue my calling?

Take time in your coaching sessions to think through these questions with your disciple-leader. Explore the various passions that God has placed in their heart; have them share what they have heard from friends, family members, and trusted advisers; and discuss opportunities that God has provided to pursue this passion. Once we understand what God has called us to do, we can set our goals and steps of action to fulfill what God has called us to do for his glory.

GOALS

Goals are those "big" items a leader needs to accomplish in order to achieve the mission God has given them with the community of believers God has placed alongside them in mission. It is here that a coach is often able to help a disciple find some clarity by prioritizing the goals that are truly needed to follow God's calling.

A woman once told one of our coaching associates that she felt that one of her goals was to organize the church office for efficiency and productivity. The problem was that her assigned responsibility at the church was to organize and manage the community groups. As important as it is to have an efficient office, her calling (community groups) had nothing to do with that stated goal. Jesus Christ has called each of us to "make disciples of all nations, baptizing them in the name of the Father and of the Son and of the Holy Spirit, teaching them to observe all that I have commanded you" (Matthew 28:18–20). In light of this calling that God has given to every believer, we must determine specifically how we are called by God to make disciples. Is it through music or athletics or church planting or serving the homeless? Knowing our specific calling will help determine our goals — both long-term goals and incremental, short-term goals that will help us achieve the long-term goals.

For instance, a man may feel called to plant a church in San Francisco. His call, verified by his passion for reaching the lost in San Francisco, affirmed by the people in his life who are closest to him, and confirmed by the place he is in — the opportunities available to him right now — will determine his goal. Still, he may have a series of short-term goals to accomplish before he can reach his long-term goal. He may sense a need to get married. He may need to raise money. He may need to finish his education. He may need to relocate to the Bay Area. He will need to determine what his short-term goals, also called "operational goals," are in order to accomplish his long-term goals. What matters most is that he determines his goals based on his calling by God.

I often describe goals as the "big buckets" that God has assigned each of us to carry on our journey. To complete the journey, we must intentionally concentrate most of our time and energy on those few buckets. As we begin carrying buckets that are not fulfilling our God-given calling, we neglect the big-goal buckets. Then, instead of doing one or two things well, we end up trying to do many things — and our results are just mediocre, bearing little fruit for the kingdom. The worst thing a person can do is to avoid what God has called you to do. This is why it is just as important to identify which buckets to *ignore* as it is to identify which buckets to focus on. Once you identify the buckets God is calling you to concentrate on, you begin filling these buckets through action steps. It is important to keep Proverbs 16:9 in view as you set goals: "The heart of man plans his way, but the LORD establishes his steps." Paul's Macedonian call included original plans that were thwarted by the Spirit (Acts 16:6–10). Goals are necessary, but calling is better. Goals fail often. Goals must submit to calling.

A coach can keep a disciple-leader focused on the essential goals that are necessary to answer God's call. Some leaders will tend to be long on vision and dreams and will have grand goals, but they'll fall short on strategic implementation or steps of action. Ambition without implementation will lead to frustration and apathy. This is why the next segment is necessary. A disciple must develop specific action steps to complete the goals they have set to follow God's call.

STEPS OF ACTION

A calling determines a goal, but specific steps of action are still needed to accomplish these goals. Too often, a person focuses on the steps of action that are right before them and loses connection back to the goals and back to God's calling on their life. Corporations employ strategic management teams to evaluate their business with regard to its mission, vision, and goals. Coaching applies this same idea by reinforcing steps of action that are directly connected to accomplishing mission-based goals. Our disciple-leaders benefit from regular monitoring to determine if they are effectively accomplishing the goals God has called them to pursue.

A woman with three young kids at home may have a goal of keeping some semblance of sanity in her home. She dutifully feeds them and provides educational stimulus and recreational opportunities; she keeps them healthy with proper hygiene and with medication as needed. She spends sixteen to eighteen hours a day serving the needs of her children, her home, and her husband. But inside, she is miserable and depressed and tired most of the time. It may be that she is simply disorganized, or perhaps she lacks clear steps of action to know how to care for her children in her home—steps that are based on her goal and are driven by her calling. Her real goal, the one she defaults to without intentionality, may simply be to survive rather than grabbing hold of the goal that matches her calling, namely, raising godly children who love God, serve him, and glorify him. She will be continually frustrated if she fails to tie her menial steps of action to her calling. This is why we must regularly review our action steps to faithfully pursue what God has called us to do. A gospel coach helps a disciple-leader by walking them through this ongoing review.

STEWARDSHIP

A leader bogs down when they run out of time, resources, energy, ideas, knowledge, skill, or motivation. When that happens, they typically focus on their deficit. In order to accomplish what God has called this person to do, they must employ a whole-life stewardship that serves God's call. Some people have great self-discipline in their life, but they use it to serve their own preferences, the idols they have made of a secure or comfortable life. The gospel reminds us that we are stewards — that all we have is a gift of God's undeserved grace — and as such we are managers of the property of another person. The Scriptures repeatedly teach us that "our" gifts, abilities, passion, knowledge, skills, and calling have been entrusted to us by God in order to glorify him in everything we do.

- "Every good gift and every perfect gift is from above, coming down from the Father of lights with whom there is no variation or shadow due to change" (James 1:17).
- "Moreover, it is required of stewards that they be found trustworthy" (1 Corinthians 4:2).
- "So, whether you eat or drink, or whatever you do, do all to the glory of God" (1 Corinthians 10:31).
- "And whatever you do, in word or deed, do everything in the name of the Lord Jesus, giving thanks to God the Father through him" (Colossians 3:17).

You may notice that I'm using stewardship in a slightly different way than many people do. As we have seen, our calling by God leads to the establishment of goals in which we seek to accomplish the mission with God's people for which he has called us. Those goals then lead to steps of action, and what we are talking about now is *how to implement these steps of action with a stewardship mind-set.*

Stewardship is not just a matter of spending our money. It involves making responsible decisions about every area of our life—our time, our resources, our energy, our walk with God, our health, our marriage, our family, our finances, our career, and our gifts and abilities. Our calling from God drives a whole-life stewardship approach. In fact, one of the most evident fruits of a gospel life plan is faithful stewardship of our lives for the glory of God.

Stewardship is not just managing, but investing every area of our lives in response to the good news. The apostle Peter states the following:

> As each has received a gift, use it to serve one another, as good stewards of God's varied grace: whoever speaks, as one who speaks oracles of God; whoever serves, as one who serves by the strength that God supplies—in order that in everything God may be glorified through Jesus Christ. To him belong glory and dominion forever and ever. Amen.
>
> —1 Peter 4:10–11

Whole-life stewardship is making wise decisions about how to most effectively use our opportunities for the glory of God.

Stewardship includes removing the distractions in our lives that keep us from accomplishing our God-given goals. I have an eye chart prominently displayed in my office. It gets people's attention almost immediately because they rightly assume that I am *not* an optometrist. When they ask me about the eye chart, and they usually do, I talk about how we have to see the "Big E" on the eye chart before we move down the rows to read the letters with incrementally smaller fonts. I share how the chart reminds me that my "Big E" is leading global churches to plant global churches and that I can't squint at other things unless that is done well. If they are still interested (or, more likely, as they stare at me blankly), I ask them what their "Big E" is.

The truth is that it takes guts to stop doing some things you are currently doing so that you can do something else well. Stewardship involves intentionally ignoring some things so you can keep your eye on the main thing that God is calling you to focus on. You have to ask yourself what is sucking resources away from accomplishing your God-given calling. Jesus wants us to be a shining light for him so that all can see and give glory to God (Matthew 5:16). We can set a thousand different lights along a mile-long road, or we can take that same amount of electrical energy and concentrate it into a single laser beam and accomplish something significant. God has entrusted gifts to us to steward for his glory and others' good (Matthew 25:14–30). We will be held accountable for what we do with what we are given, so we must seek to avoid squandering these gifts through a lack of focus.

Coaches can help disciple-leaders to properly steward the following areas of life so that they can strategically fulfill the goals that God has called them to accomplish:

1. *Abilities.* God has given each of us unique abilities—physically, mentally, emotionally, and relationally. Paul reminded Timothy not to neglect the gift that he was given and to fan into flame this gift of God (1 Timothy 4:14; 2 Timothy 1:6). We must coach our disciple-leaders to recognize their unique abilities as we lead them to steward them well.

2. *Knowledge.* Because people do not know what to do with the knowledge that God has given them, they do not steward their knowledge toward that which God has called them. We aren't called to amass knowledge and experience; we are called to invest it in others for God's glory.

3. *Money.* God has entrusted each of us with financial resources. In the Gospels (Matthew 25:14–30; Luke 19:12–27), Jesus tells the parable of the talents in which the master does not judge the three servants on the basis of the amount of money they were entrusted with, but rather on how they utilized that money for the advancement of the kingdom. I'm afraid that most of us are like the one-talent servant who did not put to use the resources entrusted to him. The first two servants quickly put their master's money to good use. They were rewarded as "good and faithful servants," their responsibility in their master's service increased, and they shared in their master's joy. I find that too many church leaders spend their money but do not steward their money with their whole-life calling in mind.

4. *Relationships.* According to Jesus, the second greatest com-

mandment is to "love your neighbor as yourself" (Matthew 22:37–39). The greatest commandment is, of course, to love God. One way we love people is to go and make disciples of all nations. Another way we love people is by serving them. Jesus illustrated this in his life on earth. He proclaimed the good news with compassion and love, and he served others as he pointed to the graciousness of God. A gospel coach helps the disciple-leader to steward relationships, utilize them for the glory of God (including positions of authority), and seek to restore broken relationships.

5. *Time.* Every person I have ever coached has struggled with time management. Unlike almost every other resource, everyone has the *same* amount of time—168 hours a week. The problem is that we try to manage our time instead of properly stewarding our time through the filter of our calling. Not having enough time is never the problem; stewarding and prioritizing is. You can't manage time; you *invest* it. For instance, if I know I am called by God to pastor a church in a vocational manner, then I must set aside forty to fifty hours a week to faithfully serve that congregation. But I must also weigh the other areas to which God has called me. If he has called me to be a spouse or writer or parent, or to serve in any other capacity (soccer coach, community group leader, and so forth), then I must factor that in as I steward my time for the glory of God. I can't do everything. So I must invest first in the areas to which God has called me. As I coach men, the problem is usually threefold: they think they can do more than they are able; they are not strategic about investing their time in pursuing their objectives; and they are not clear about God's calling in their life.

Stewarding Time

Stewardship of time seems to be one of the more difficult areas of a person's life to develop wisely. Time must be a servant to the calling of a person's life. Your calling cannot be a servant to time. Traditional time management theory suggests that by doing things more efficiently, you'll eventually gain control of your life, and this increased control will bring personal fulfillment. But increased efficiency does not necessarily help facilitate the objectives that lead to the fulfilling of your calling. Instead, it may be helpful to answer the following questions:

1. What are my stated goals?
2. What do I actually do with my time?
3. What is most important in my life to do?
4. What can I eliminate from my life that is taking time away from doing the most important things?

Most Christian leaders have not been equipped with basic time stewardship skills. And yet, in the business world, it is unusual to lack basic training in efficient use of time. Corporations like Hewlett-Packard, Ford, General Dynamics, Eastman Kodak, Coca Cola, IBM, and AT&T spend hundreds of thousands of dollars every year so that their employees will have basic time management training. Some church leaders stubbornly push against these and consider them unbiblical tools. But consider the cost of not managing your time and life well. The list may include the following:

1. loss of personal growth (spiritually, emotionally, physically, academically)
2. loss of creativity
3. loss of perspective (rushed, hurried, adrenaline, rage)
4. loss of productivity
5. loss of family time
6. loss of honoring God with your time
7. loss of fulfilling your calling

Some authorities tell us there is a serious energy crisis on the earth. Still other authorities tell us there are many energy resources that we haven't even touched yet. It all seems to boil down to how are we using or not using the earth's vast energy resources. The same thing is true of many people in the church. They are experiencing a serious energy crisis in their lives. Some of them keep doing more, working harder, and accomplishing less. They feel exhausted. Others are going back and forth between periods of extreme highs and periods of having no energy at all. Some leaders are totally exhausted and depressed at all times. Business expert Peter Drucker said he has yet to see an executive, regardless of his or her position, who could not get rid of 25 percent of the demands on his time without anybody noticing. In other words, most of us should be able to eliminate 25 percent of what we do with our time without it having a detrimental impact on our work.

To help us further explore ways of stewarding our time, let's look at seven external time wasters and six internal time wasters.

SEVEN EXTERNAL TIME WASTERS

1. *Personal interruptions.* This is one of the first time wasters we often encounter. How can we effectively steward our time to avoid these interruptions? Above all, be firm. When someone asks you if you "have a minute," ask about their agenda and see if there are other people who might be able to talk to them. Block out time to focus for long periods of time on the

Personal Energy Stewardship

It might be beneficial to check your "personal energy stewardship." Score yourself honestly on a scale of 1 to 5 (1 = never; 2 = rarely; 3 = sometimes; 4 = often; 5 = always) in each question. A score above 35 is cause for concern about your energy stewardship.

1. Are my emotions dictated by my personal energy?
2. Is my life running on energy that I siphon from other life-giving people?
3. Is my life running on crisis energy (lack of sleep, overtime)?
4. Is my life running on addiction energies (caffeine, sugar)?
5. Are certain people or certain projects in my life draining my energy?
6. Is my energy gas tank consistently on empty?
7. Am I lacking focus when attempting projects?

8. Do I lack motivation to get up in the morning?
9. Do I dread relationships that require extra effort?
10. Do I waste time with mindless activities?

most important things in your life. If you work with others in an office setting, agree on a "quiet hour" in which you do not interrupt each other.

2. *Phone calls and text messages.* Learn to set a callback time for phone messages, and use voice mail options if they are available. With cell phones, this is an even bigger challenge. In the past, receptionists were able to filter incoming calls and take messages. Now, with text messaging, Skype, and the countless number of people who have your cell phone number, it is tempting to answer every incoming call and immediately view every incoming text. Realize that you may have to overcome guilt feelings if you ignore a call.

3. *E-mail barrages.* Along with phone calls and texts, most of us struggle to deal with a horde of e-mails every day. Use your e-mail tools to screen for junk messages. Unsubscribe from unwanted e-mail lists. Schedule two to three times a day to check and respond to e-mails — and then stick to your rule. Ongoing e-mail work distracts you and keeps you from being productive. When you do tackle your e-mail, learn to use the two-minute rule. If you can handle the e-mail within two minutes, do it; if not, file it and schedule a later time to deal with it. You need only two digital file folders to manage your email: an "Answer" file to answer later (requiring more than two minutes), and a "Mail" file in which all of the incoming or sent messages that you absolutely need to keep are kept. Don't be an e-mail hoarder. You can digitally search more efficiently this way. Delete all other e-mails. Strive to have an empty in-box at the end of each day.

4. *Message alerts and phone ringers.* Let me suggest turning off the message alert on your e-mail to keep you from losing your focus. When working on important projects, turn off your phone ringer. Put a sign on your closed door that reads, "I'm working on an important deadline. I'll be free at 3:15 p.m."

5. *Short attention spans.* We must learn to focus. Some find it helpful to use instrumental music or white noise to help quiet their

mind while working. Use headphones to block out noise when working in a busy place. Set up your workspace so that your back is to the traffic flow if you are easily distracted.

6. *Social media.* This is an area of distraction that is increasingly common today. Twitter and Facebook have added a new doorway into leaders' lives that can cause constant interruptions. Social media is an important portal for communicating and leading, but it comes with added pressure to respond to others' posts and updates. Learn to be proactive in your social media engagement rather than reacting to every comment made on your social media account. Use it as a tool and not as an open door for interruptions. I set aside a total of five minutes a day for Facebook and two minutes for Twitter.

7. *Your daily energy cycles.* Be aware of how your workflow affects your energy level, and decide on the best time of the day to tackle an important project. I block out every morning until noon as mental time to think and brainstorm because this is when I think best. I save my afternoons for more relationally oriented activities such as answering e-mails, responding to coaching opportunities, and attending meetings. You will have to determine your own energy cycle.

Six Internal Time Wasters

In addition to the seven external time wasters, there are six internal factors that affect our stewardship of time:

1. *Lack of delegation.* This time waster is especially common among younger leaders, who can easily get locked into the trap of thinking they have to do everything themselves. The truth is that God has equipped you to do some things very well, and in those places where you are not equipped to do things well, he will usually give you other people to do that work. You can easily be robbed of time by failing to delegate or by delegating responsibility without giving the needed authority to complete the work without your input or approval.

2. *The "tyranny of the urgent."* Some young leaders are just wired to be impatient. When they think of something, they believe it has to be done right now. Every e-mail does not need to be answered right now—or ever, in some cases. Not every demand that comes in needs to be addressed. Good leadership involves learning how to properly

filter all of the noises around you—complaints, e-mails, interruptions, demands, and even fun opportunities. Charles Hummel gives wise teaching in his book on this subject:

> Many important tasks need not be done today, or even this week ... But often urgent, though less important, tasks call for immediate response—endless demands pressure every waking hour ... The appeal of these demands seems irresistible, and they devour our energy. But in the light of eternity their momentary prominence fades. With a sense of loss we recall the important tasks that have been shunted aside. We realize that we've become slaves to the tyranny of the urgent.[90]

3. *Procrastination*. It should come as no surprise to any of us that procrastination ranks high on the list of major time wasters. Unpleasant tasks will often be avoided deliberately. People who habitually procrastinate usually become prone to interruptions and actually find a way to invite them.

4. *Perfectionism*. On the other hand, a tendency toward perfectionism can be equally problematic. Instead of putting off a project, we end up spending far too much time on different projects. While we should all have a commitment to pursue excellence, sometimes this can be taken too far and result in a serious waste of time as we neglect to spend time on more critical areas. Some people obsess over perfection and as a result have a difficult time ever considering a project "complete."

5. *Lack of planning*. This is another common reason that time ends up being wasted. Good leaders must learn to plan ahead. I suggest to those whom I coach that they take the following blocks of time to plan ahead:

- daily (30 minutes)
- weekly (1 hour)
- monthly (1/2 day)
- quarterly (1 day)
- yearly (2 to 3 days)

Planning your goals and action steps in distinct blocks of time helps in setting deadlines and can be an excellent way of making yourself accountable to meeting your goals.

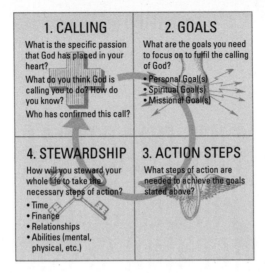

Figure 10: Gospel Life Plan (revisited)

6. *Lack of a gospel life plan.* Closely related to a lack of planning is the very problem we have been talking about in this chapter—having no clear calling, no goals that are inspired and connected to that calling, and no specific action steps that are stewarded well. This may be the greatest time waster of all, but it is also the easiest one to miss. That is why I challenge every coach and every disciple-leader to spend time working on a gospel life plan.

CHAPTER 12

FIVE PRACTICAL PHASES OF THE COACHING SESSION

NOW THAT WE HAVE much of the gospel coaching foundation laid, all that remains is to examine the actual coaching session. The time that you spend together should be an extension of your theology, expressed in practical fashion, for the purpose of building healthy disciples and healthy, reproductive churches. We suggest using the acronym CROSS as a model for remembering the flow of the coaching conversation. This acronym has the added benefit of reminding the coach to remain connected to the cross—the emblem of the gospel story.

The coaching session, following the CROSS model, is broken up into five phases:

- **C**–Connect
- **R**–Review
- **O**–Objectives
- **S**–Strategies
- **S**–Supplication and Spirit

A coaching session, lasting anywhere from forty-five to sixty minutes and meeting either every other week or monthly, starts the metaphorical hiking journey at the trailhead. The trailhead is where the coach and disciple relationally engage and determine their destination for that session. The destination must be identified early in their time together in order for the session to be effective. It is not imperative that every coaching session arrives at the end goal within the time allotted, but without a destination, the coaching session will be unfocused and lack purpose.

These destinations can be simple or complex—as simple as determining an exercise regimen for the next six months, or as complex as planting a new church in a city a thousand miles away in the next twelve months. The "destination" for the coaching session might be a goal in a disciple-leader's personal, spiritual, or missional life. The journey taken during the session will likely have many twists and turns, as ideas and concepts are considered and challenges faced. Along the way, the guiding principle will be the gospel, as the coach addresses the various ideas and challenges that come up in the course of the conversation through the lens of the gospel message. They will seek to shepherd the disciple and not just get them to the goal as quickly as possible. A coach and disciple will always need to identify one or two clearly defined objectives for their coaching session. As you can see (Figure 11), the sign near the mountains indicates this objective for the session—the destination you are heading toward together.

From the parking lot (the trailhead), a coach seeks to know the disciple, and then, based on their conversation, they will attempt to lead the disciple toward their agreed-on session objectives, all the while speaking the truth in love (Ephesians 4:15). As the trail is traversed, and issues and problems and challenges are addressed, the coach feeds the disciple with scriptural principles to nourish the disciple's quest to follow God's will. Finally, the coach protects the disciple from choosing a path that may hinder the pursuit of the calling that God had aroused within them. The coach provides a protective guardrail, as it were. It is here that the coach rebukes, affirms, corrects, and encourages the disciple

Figure 11: Coaching Journey Illustration

in their pursuit of God's calling. In subsequent coaching sessions, the coach will protect the disciple by holding them accountable for the decisions they have made in accordance with God's call on the disciple's life.

As with any other journey, new paths are discovered and discussed. It may be appropriate at times to stop and rest along the journey. At these times other aspects of a person's life may need to be explored and examined. The conversation may expose a sin that has lain dormant prior to the session. It is appropriate in these circumstances not to push on toward the goal, but rather to create a new coaching objective of addressing the sin issue before pressing on. It may also be appropriate at this juncture to stop and feed on spiritual truths or to examine a passage of Scripture or for the coach to encourage or affirm the disciple on the journey.

The disciple's compass or GPS (global positioning system) is his gospel life plan. It monitors the calling, goals, action steps, and stewardship. It may need to be referenced at various times in the coaching journey. In other words, always keep the compass handy to provide direction and to keep you from veering off the path leading toward your objective.

C – CONNECT

As we have repeatedly emphasized, the first part of any gospel coaching session involves connecting. There are three key ways in which a disciple and coach must connect: to one another, to the gospel, and to the Holy Spirit.

CONNECT TO EACH OTHER

A shepherd must get to know their sheep. The coach and disciple-leader must have a good relationship to experience effective coaching outcomes. Let me stress this again: A good relationship may be the number one criterion for effective coaching relationships. In the early stages, a coach will need to work hard at developing this connection. A coach cares about the disciple as a person and not just as a professional. To accomplish this, a coach must ask good questions and listen well to the answers because the person is a fellow heir of the grace of God. A gospel coach asks questions in the three main aspects of the disciple's life in a relational manner. Use the questions in this book and spend at least the first five minutes connecting to each other to get to know the disciple-leader in a personal, spiritual, and missional way.

CONNECT TO THE GOSPEL

In addition to connecting to one another, the coach and disciple must connect to the gospel. It is imperative that the coach communicates with the gospel, through the gospel, and in full understanding of the gospel. Otherwise, the coaching relationship may be reduced to the dispensing of clever ideas, worldly counsel, and gut feelings. Since humanity has deviated from God's original intention for human life, we suffer the effects of our sin and brokenness, both in ourselves and in our relationships with others. We can see these effects in increasing numbers of people struggling with depression, burnout, anxiety, fear, and self-centered behavioral problems. We see it affecting our relationships with others and society at large through increased sexual exploitation and violence, war, and oppression of the poor. The only antidote to the personal and communal effects of our sin is the gospel. In their book *Counsel from the Cross*, Elyse Fitzpatrick and Dennis Johnson remind us of this truth:

The cross of Christ and the gospel that proclaims it really are "the power of God for salvation [comprehensive rescue] to everyone who believes" (Romans 1:16). On that cross, on which occurred the execution of God's Son, lies hidden "the power of God and the wisdom of God" (1 Corinthians 1:18–24). And in that cross lies the power both to liberate hearts caught in seemingly unbreakable cycles of defeat and to instill hope that *change can actually happen* in us and in those whom we love fiercely and resent intensely at the same time.[1]

We justly deserve the punishment for our sin — the wrath of God that Jesus bore in our place on the cross. The cross confronts and destroys our sinful pride and self-sufficiency. It humbles us and sets us free from our sin and our idolatry. We can no longer stand in smug self-righteousness, looking down at others with condescension. At the same time, as we kneel in humble awareness of our sins before a holy God, the cross reminds us that we are deeply loved by God. We are loved in a way that is beyond our understanding, not because we deserve this love, but because God *is* love. In Christ, God justly condemns our sin while declaring us his beloved. Our sin is seen for what it is — far worse than we could have imagined. At the same time, we see that we are more loved than we could have ever realized. This is the gospel that we desperately need.

The gospel is the centering factor of everything that is proclaimed and the filter through which everything else is passed. Coaching without the gospel will only produce self-affection, self-indulgence, self-confidence, self-satisfaction, and self-redemption.

CONNECT TO THE HOLY SPIRIT

In addition to connecting relationally and to the gospel, a connection must be made with the Spirit of God. We must invite and be utterly dependent on the Spirit of God to enlighten our spirit to connect with the needs of the disciple we are coaching. We can grow in our skills as a coach by the regenerative Spirit of God. The apostle Paul urges us to pray at all times in the Spirit for ourselves and for others so that we may be able to communicate the gospel boldly (Ephesians 6:18–20). If you are going to coach others toward the gospel, then the Spirit of God must be invading your life and interrupting your life as you walk in a coaching journey with others in obedience to the call of God in their life for the glory of God. It is the work of the Spirit rather than our abilities to coach that produces Christlikeness (2 Corinthians 3:18; Galatians 5:16; 1 Peter 1:2).

The coach reminds the church leader that by the Spirit, the gospel has given them a new power, not only to understand God's will, but also to do God's will (Philippians 2:13). It will be by this Spirit applying the gospel that they will continue to grow in grace (Romans 5:5; Galatians 5:22–23), to minister in confidence despite their weakness (2 Corinthians 3:5–6), and be bold in their witness (Acts 4:31; 7:54–60). After relationally connecting, ask the disciple to open the session in prayer and invite the Spirit and the gospel to consume your coaching session.

R – REVIEW

In the review phase, the coach and the disciple can identify which specific objective they believe the Spirit of God is urging them to focus on for the coaching session. Coaches help others get where they're going; they help people find their way and give them a sense of perspective. Bob Logan rightly stated, "Within the framework of a coaching relationship, people can take stock of where they are, figure out where God wants them to go, and decide what steps to get there."[2] I (Scott) have developed an Internet-based tool (www. GospelCoach.com) that can assist you in reviewing the questions you wish to discuss and even have answers to those questions submitted prior to the session. This keeps a record of your sessions together and helps you and your disciple remember to discuss any issues that were not completely covered in past sessions and then choose which one or two objectives to discuss in your next session.

The review phase reflects on past sessions and agreements that have been made. One of the functions of a coach is to provide feedback. Paul Stanley and Robert Clinton highlight the importance of this review for giving evaluated feedback:

A key to good coaching is observation, feedback, and evaluation. An experienced coach does not try to control the player, but rather seeks to inspire and equip him with the necessary motivation, perspective, and skills to enable him to excellent performance and effectiveness. A coach understands that experience is the teaching vehicle, but a wise coach knows the power of evaluated experience.[3]

The review phase should always include a celebration of God's grace in the disciple's life. We strongly encourage intentional pursuit of a culture that recognizes the evidences of God's grace in our life. If we don't recognize the evidences of God's grace in our lives, then we are self-centered and, as a result, not cross-centered. Most of us are more aware of the absence of God than the presence of God. We are prone to take God's grace for granted and therefore miss out on an opportunity to give God glory.

I have found that most church leaders fail to see the evidence of God's grace and thus fail to celebrate God's acts of mercy and affection for them in spite of their rebellious hearts and attitudes. I was coaching a church planter, and we were discussing his four-month-old church plant. About seventy people were attending the church gathering each week, and the church was in the process of training leaders and experiencing transformation. But in the coaching session, I kept hearing him whine about how little was being accomplished, how terrible some of the leaders were, and how frustrated he was. Every question I asked him stimulated this complaining spirit. So in an attempt to identify the evidences of God's grace, even when things are going bad (*especially* when things are going bad), I asked him to list ten things to celebrate — great things that were happening in his personal life, spiritual life, or missional life. He didn't want to do it, but I told him I couldn't coach him effectively unless he completed this task. A month later, his wife contacted me and thanked me again and again for forcing him to see how much he was blessed. She said that he was miserable to live with and that this "kick in the pants" helped him to see the many things that are worth celebrating.

To see evidences of God's grace, one could start by reflecting on the list of fruit of the Spirit (Galatians 5:22–23). How has God demonstrated himself through the fruit flourishing in your life? How have others illuminated the gospel through demonstrations of the fruit of the Spirit? You may find evidences of God's grace in places you've never looked.

1. love (1 Corinthians 13:4–8; 1 John 4:16)
2. joy (Nehemiah 8:10; Hebrews 12:2)
3. peace (Romans 5:1; 15:13)
4. patience, or long-suffering (Ephesians 4:2; Colossians 1:11)
5. kindness (2 Corinthians 6:6-7)
6. goodness (Ephesians 5:9; 2 Thessalonians 1:11)
7. faithfulness (Isaiah 25:1; Ephesians 3:16–17)
8. gentleness, or meekness (Galatians 6:1; Ephesians 4:2)
9. self-control, or temperance (2 Peter 1:5–7)

We must remember that it is important to celebrate God's grace. Celebrating what God is accomplishing and is graciously allowing a disciple to participate in guards against self-accomplishment and entitlement. In addition to celebrating evidences of God's grace, the review phase explores the issues the disciple is facing in their personal, spiritual, or missional life. If past assignments were given, review the progress. Review any unfulfilled accountability agreements as well.

If a disciple hasn't been able to follow through on what the Spirit is calling the disciple to do, the coach must determine the appropriate steps. Did they lack the needed resources? Can the coach point them to people or materials to help? Does the disciple need a rebuke or affirmation? Does the disciple lack an understanding of the process of objectives and stewardship? Do they lack a skill, or is it a motivational issue? Was there something else the coach needed to discuss with them? Ken Blanchard believes that providing feedback is the most cost-effective strategy for improving performance and instilling satisfaction.[4] Many people only offer critiques behind a person's back, which is unhelpful. The coach is expected to give *honest* feedback.

A faithful coach assists the disciple in closing the learning gap between the current reality and their potential. The coach might assist the planter in reviewing the picture of the ministry as they see it in future years. The disciple needs to know whether or not they have met their key objectives from the previous session and that the coach believes in them. The review phase examines where a disciple is on the journey toward the major objectives they believe God is calling them to pursue and what the next steps would be to get there.

O–OBJECTIVE

The next piece in the CROSS coaching journey is for the disciple-leader to identify the *major objective* for the coaching session. An objective, for our purposes, is "a clearly defined, desired outcome in a given coaching session, determined by the coach and the disciple, to fulfill God's calling for the disciple." If an objective is not determined, the coaching session may be pleasant but very little will be accomplished. It is not advisable to allow for more than a couple objectives in a single coaching session.

As mentioned earlier, when I coach others, I picture a mountain peak, with a winding road leading up to the mountain. I often draw it out on a blank piece of paper. On the signpost near the mountain peak (see Figure 11), I write in the objective for the session. The objective might be "to establish small groups in the church" or it might be "to lose ten pounds" or "to plan for a women's Bible study." Then, for that portion of our coaching session, we focus on that one objective. We have a destination in mind, and we begin walking up the trail toward it.

Questions to stimulate this part of the coaching conversation include the following:

- What are the most important objectives you need to work on this month? Why do you see them as the most important?
- Have you looked at the mission lately? What aspect of your mission demands the highest priority now? Why? How will addressing this priority help you implement the mission God has called you to?
- How is your community playing a part in your goals?
- What potential obstacles are blocking the way to accomplishing one or all of the goals?

When you construct a building, it is important to observe the proper order of construction: blueprint, engineering, foundation, plumbing, floors, walls, roof, electricity, doors. In a similar way, helping leaders to set good goals in the proper order can be one of the most beneficial gifts a coach gives. It is vital for the leader to see the importance of each objective and clearly agree to what needs to be done. All leaders will get stuck by virtue of the enormity of the mission and their ambition. Sometimes they lose sight of the original calling. Other times the mission is being swallowed up by the urgent and unimportant. The benefit of a coach is found in their ability to objectively observe and make recommendations.

S – STRATEGIES

The first *S* stands for "Strategies." Strategies are concerned with the practical means and plans for achieving the objective. Each objective will have specific strategies associated with it. Strategies are the specific individual steps and action-oriented, measurable tasks to accomplish the objective. On the metaphorical coaching trail, the initial step is to determine where the disciple is. It is a "You Are Here" orientation. You have to know where the person is before you can lead them to the objective.

In a recent coaching session, one of my disciple-leaders mentioned that he wanted to establish small groups in his church. After further inquiry, I discovered that he had no groups currently in place, that he had one leader, and that he had no training resources. I asked him what plans he had to reach his objective. He mentioned three specific things. I wrote those down on the handwritten "journey page" as supporting strategies. Then I asked him what obstacles he anticipated facing along this journey. He mentioned four specific things, which I drew as big rocks standing in the way of navigating toward the objective. Before he established small groups, he had to address these obstacles. We spent the rest of the session discussing how to traverse over, around, or through the big rocks. It is important to note that we didn't reach the objective in a single coaching session, but we had a destination in mind. In the next session, we reviewed the progress and picked up where we had left off. He had worked on some of the obstacles in between our coaching sessions.

A coach may ask the following questions to stimulate strategic planning:

- What types of things will you do to accomplish your objective?
- What are you going to do first? When will you start? When will you have it done?
- Whom do you need to help you accomplish the tasks?
- What can I do to help you stay focused on the task?
- How does the strategy advance the gospel orientation of your mission? Are your strategies clear enough?
- Have you identified all of the obstacles in reaching your objective?

SMART STRATEGIES

Objectives will be effective if they possess the following attributes of the acrostic SMART (adapted from the traditional goal-setting model that became popular in the 1980s):

- **Specific.** Be clear about what, where, when, and how. Objectives should be written in one sentence and be clear and specific enough so that anyone reading it can understand it.
- **Measurable.** Your objectives should be stated in such a way that the reader can tell that the results can be measured either quantifiably (by numbers, figures, or cost) or qualitatively (participant levels of satisfaction, improvements or expansion of services or programs, development of new skills among staff and volunteers, and so forth).
- **Aspiring.** Is it "faith based," or is it something you can do on your own? Is it what Christ wants you to do, or is it something that seems practical or reasonable? Can it be done in your own power?
- **Results focused.** What outcome are you hoping to achieve through this? How does this relate to your calling?
- **Time frame.** State a clear begin date and targeted completion time/date. Be sure to give yourself enough time to finish.

BRAINSTORMING

To assist in the strategic planning process, try brainstorming. Brainstorming, when used in a coaching session, can help the disciple-leader come up with solutions or strategies to help meet the objective that God has called them to accomplish. The goal of brainstorming is to come up with ideas and thoughts (and these may at first seem to be a bit crazy). The aim is that some of these ideas can be crafted into solutions or strategies to the problem you're trying to solve or the objective you're trying to accomplish.

During brainstorming sessions, criticism of ideas is not helpful. You are trying to open up possibilities and break down wrong or unhelpful assumptions about the limits of the problem. Judgments and in-depth analysis at this stage inhibit idea generation. To run a brainstorming session effectively within the coaching environment, try the following:

1. Appoint the coach to record all ideas that come from the session.
2. Clearly define the problem you want solved and lay out any criteria to be met. Make it clear that the objective of the meeting is to generate as many ideas as possible.
3. Encourage developing another person's ideas. Look for ways to use other ideas to create new ones.
4. Encourage an enthusiastic, uncritical attitude in the exercise. Criticism at this stage stifles creativity and cripples the free-flowing nature of a good brainstorming session.
5. Have fun! Come up with as many ideas as possible, from solidly practical ones to wildly impractical ones. Welcome creativity!
6. Ensure that no train of thought is followed for too long. Make sure that you generate a sufficient number of different ideas and that you explore individual ideas in detail.
7. Keep the major objective (big bucket) in mind as you offer ideas.

Ideas should only be evaluated *at the end* of the brainstorming session. This is the time to explore solutions further by using conventional approaches and evaluation principles.

S – SUPPLICATION AND SPIRIT

The second and final *S* in the CROSS approach to the coaching journey stands for "Supplication and Spirit." The coaching session starts with a relational convergence of Spirit and gospel and ends the same way. Supplication — or prayer — is not just an added phase to conclude a coaching session, like a perfunctory prayer at the end of a meal. Rather, it serves both as an indication of the issues in a disciple's life that concern them most deeply and as an opportunity to pray together to realign our mind, focus, and dependence on a sovereign God and an empowering Spirit. Ample time should be reserved for praying together. Through prayer, the coach may simply ask, "How can I be praying for you?" At other times, the coach may ask about more specific prayer needs as they relate to personal, spiritual, and missional life.

This phase is another way to learn about the greatest needs in a person's life. A coach may not have asked a question in the session that pertained to the area about which the disciple was most concerned. Be sure to consider the prayer request thoughtfully. It may mean that the entire coaching session is focused on just one issue — the one exposed in a prayer request.

Pray with an impassioned spirit and pray in the power of the Spirit. The noted theologian J. I. Packer contends that praying in the Spirit includes four things:

1. accessing God through Christ in one Spirit (Ephesians 2:18)
2. adoring God and thanking him for his acceptance through Christ and for the knowledge that our prayers are heard through Christ
3. requesting the Spirit's help to see and do what brings glory to Christ (Romans 8:26–27, 34)
4. requesting the Spirit to lead us to concentrate on God and his glory in Christ with a sustained, single-minded simplicity of attention and intensity of desire.[5]

The prayer phase with our disciple is a passionate petitioning of God through the Spirit and the Son to bring glory to his name.

The Supplication and Spirit phase also includes conviction by the Holy Spirit, to which we respond in faith. The disciple reflects back on the coaching conversation and identifies areas in which the Holy Spirit is leading them to repent and to come into conformity with the gospel. These can be as simple as, "I need to begin showing appreciation to my spouse," or they can be more serious, such as, "I have allowed my mind to engage in impure thoughts, and I need to confess them to my spouse and to bring my thoughts captive to the obedience of Christ."

ACCOUNTABILITY AGREEMENTS

The final aspect of the coaching session is the "accountability agreement." This is a way to keep an ongoing record of specific responses in accordance with the repentance agreed on by the disciple or of assignments given by the coach. In the Internet application at www.GospelCoach.com, these accountability agreements will continue to show up on the page for each coaching session until the action is completed. They include a due date and a description of exactly what needs to be done, the person to whom the task is assigned, and the details of how progress will be measured. Though utilizing the Internet application works well, this can be done just as simply with a notebook.

Obedience flows from the freedom of the gospel as we obey out of love and gratitude rather than out of fear. Steve Brown has said that obedience doesn't lead to freedom; instead, freedom leads to obedience. If we get this backwards, we lose both our freedom and, eventually, our desire to obey.[6] It is only through the freedom of the gospel that our lives will be transformed.

In the book of 1 Samuel, we read, "Has the LORD as great delight in burnt offerings and sacrifices, as in obeying the voice of the LORD? Behold, to obey is better than sacrifice, and to listen than the fat of rams" (1 Samuel 15:22). The first time I read this verse, I was astonished it was in the Bible. I had grown up in a legalistic church environment that had three prominent altars of sacrifice—tithing, church attendance, and soul winning. A close fourth was hair length for men and daily dress wearing (or, gasp, culottes) for women. As long as you showed up, paid up, handed up (tracts), and shaped up (clothing and hair), you were considered a godly Christian. This is what I call "Checklist Christianity." As a young man of twenty, I observed that many of the rule-conforming people I knew were also some of the meanest people I had ever met! How was this possible? Legalism is content to focus on the outside. It forces people to conform externally, manipulating them, intimidating them, and promising them rewards. Or it brings them under the reign of fear and gets them to conform externally to certain behaviors. But legalism doesn't transform the heart. And apart from God's grace, the human heart is "a perpetual factory of idols" (as John Calvin reminded us), not God-glorifying fruit.

Accountability agreements facilitate obedience—but it must be an obedience that is grounded in the gospel. The gospel has been described in terms of a three-step waltz: 1-2-3, 1-2-3, believe-repent-obey.[7] The first step in the gospel dance is *belief* in the gloriousness, graciousness, goodness, and greatness of God through Christ alone.

Once we believe, Christ's righteousness provides us with full forgiveness of our sins, and we are declared righteous through Christ and are then ready to repent. Change occurs after belief and repentance. Before belief happens, we are only experiencing the effects or consequences of sin and may be merely seeking to escape the consequences. We are made righteous by the death of Jesus, who paid the full price of our debt because we could not add one coin to the penalty of our sin: "For our sake he [God] made him [Jesus] to be sin who knew no sin, so that in him we might become the righteousness of God" (2 Corinthians 5:21). When we realize the gracious act of God in removing our sin and placing it on the body of Jesus, we are ready to repent. Martin Luther, in his commentary on Galatians, writes:

> So then, do we do nothing to obtain this righteousness? No, nothing at all. Perfect righteousness is to do nothing, to hear nothing, to know nothing of the law or of works, but to know and believe only that Christ has gone to the Father ... not as a judge, but is made by God our wisdom, righteousness, holiness, and redemption; in short, that he is our high priest entreating for us, and reigning over us and in us by grace ...

In [Christ's] righteousness and life I have no sin ... I am indeed a sinner as far as this present life and righteousness are concerned ... But I have another righteousness and life above this life—Christ the Son of God.[8]

We, through Christ and his work, are forgiven, accepted, freed from sin's power, adopted into his family as loved sons and daughters, and given the presence and power of the Holy Spirit. The Spirit is producing in us godly character and spiritual fruit, such as love, joy, peace, and self-control (Galatians 5:22–23). Through the Spirit, we can say yes to a forgiving, loving, redeeming, and gracious God who is transforming us—and only then can we say no to our flesh.

The second step in the gospel dance is a life of *repentance* with an ongoing realization of one's broken condition, along with the humble admission, "I cannot do this apart from Jesus." The Christian life is 1-2-3, 1-2-3, believe-repent-obey. The first or second step of a waltz is not the last time you step there in a waltz. So it is in the gospel dance. Your first step is to believe. Your second step is to repent. And you will return to these steps again and again.

Here are a few questions to help a disciple respond in repentance:

1. Where is the Holy Spirit convicting you in what we talked about in our session?
2. How is the Holy Spirit or the Word of God calling you to repent?
3. Specifically how will you respond in repentance?

Accountability is not a foolproof way to protect the disciple-leader, but it is an excellent tool to implement as you seek to shepherd. What does accountability look like? In my own life, I chose four men and asked them to help me by overseeing specific areas I had identified. What I didn't expect was that these men would also shepherd me in ways that I had never experienced. I have been enormously blessed by their investment in my life.

These men serve me well as proactive, protective barriers. For example, Mark Driscoll once posed a question, asking me what steps I was taking to prepare for the time when our children would leave home as adults. I hadn't even thought about it. Mark held me accountable to provide some ideas the next time we met. This accountability forced my wife and I to talk about a painful subject. We discussed how much we love our sons and how we subconsciously reject the idea that they may ever leave home (even though they remind us of that fact every opportunity they get). While this is a simple example, the questions and challenges these men speak into my life protect me and help me to avoid self-deception and address blind spots in my character.

My friend and leadership coach Bruce Wesley developed a series of forty leadership questions to help a coach protect a leader. I am grateful to him for sharing his list of excellent questions (you can access them in their entirety in appendix 3). They include questions about:

- self-leadership: How are you stewarding the gifts you have for the greatest benefit?
- interpersonal leadership: Do you say yes and no with clarity so that it builds confidence and trust?
- organizational leadership: What opportunities did you decline for the sake of fulfilling your objectives?
- team leadership: How do you demonstrate your love for each team member?
- pastoral leadership: How are you making disciples?

One of my greatest concerns is the number of church leaders who are falling (or, perhaps better to say, leaping) into sexual immorality. This is not a new problem. The Internet seems to have exposed to the public some of these formerly quiet indiscretions hidden behind the walls of the church. I recently spoke with two wives whose pastor husbands left them for younger women who were employed in their churches. These wives were devastated over the tragedy and filled with anxiety about how they were going to provide direction and provision for the young children at home. In both cases, the pastors had participated in their immoral behavior for an extended period of time, raising questions about their personal accountability.

One of the pastors was in regular accountability with other pastors in the church. These younger associate pastors were asking their senior pastor all the right questions, but he lied to them for seven months. Part of the problem with accountability is that it isn't always properly administered within the church. Often, men join an accountability group as a facade to hide their spiritually anemic lives. There are even some men who participate just to get their wives off their backs. The focus in these groups is on the accountability but not on *responding to the gospel*. There has to be a greater motivation for accountability than checking off a list of questions asked by men who are hoping they won't be asked the same questions.

Below are five foundations for good accountability:

1. Focus on the gospel and on your response to the grace of God. It is the love of Christ demonstrated through his death and resurrection that controls us (2 Corinthians 5:14–15).
2. Find people of your same gender who have regular contact with you and can observe your life closely.
3. Find people who are not employed by you or under your direct authority. Sometimes they may be keeping silent as a way of ensuring that they don't lose their job. It is acceptable to supplement your accountability with people under your supervision, but they cannot be the only ones holding you accountable.
4. Tell them that occasionally you may lie to them on purpose to test whether they will press you for accurate answers to their questions. Someone asked me how he could know if an accountability team was actually working for his benefit. I told him to lie to them and see if they press anyway. If a person can lie to their accountability team, it is of no value or protection to them. The point is not to cultivate a habit of lying; it's to train your accountability partners to ask hard questions and to be relentless about receiving accurate answers. Ultimately, you do this because you value honesty and are deeply aware of your own capacity for sinful deception.
5. Utilize questions that vary from week to week, and find questions that examine sins in our heads and hearts, and

not just in our hands. I believe sin starts in our hearts, and we then devise plans in our heads to fulfill them. Jesus condemned with equal force not only the act of adultery but also the conceived thoughts of adultery (Matthew 5:28). James wrote, "Each person is tempted when he is lured and enticed by his own desire. Then desire when it has conceived gives birth to sin, and sin when it is fully grown brings forth death" (James 1:14–15).

I liken accountability to a bridge over a body of water. The goal of a bridge is to get people and vehicles across water. The means of crossing the water is the bridge. The pillars uphold the bridge and are important for its structural integrity. Accountability is like the pillars of the bridge. When someone sets out to cross a bridge, they do not say, "I drove to the bridge to talk about the amazing engineering technology and to take pictures of these massive pillars of concrete and steel." Rather, they say, "I drove on the bridge so that I can cross this body of water and get to the other side." The focus is primarily on the *destination*; the method of getting there (the bridge) and the supporting structures (the pillars) are secondary. The purpose for accountability is to provide the spiritual integrity that can allow the gospel to transform every aspect of one's life. On the other side of that bridge is Christlikeness. When the focus is exclusively on accountability, it is like a Bridge to Nowhere—awesome pillars, but no destination.

I have a formalized and detailed accountability structure for my personal life, spiritual life, and missional life. Four men serve me well and ask me difficult and probing questions. They have permission to ask questions about me with my wife and my two sons. Accountability is not the silver bullet—but it *is* a bullet. It is a defense mechanism to be implemented with precision. It can be helpful when the focus is on gospel transformation and not merely on behavioral modification. Church leaders, especially, should be involved in healthy, gospel-focused accountability with others: "Ponder the path of your feet [and allow others to carefully observe your thoughts and your heart's passions]; then all your ways will be sure" (Proverbs 4:26).

A gospel coach protects a disciple by exercising biblical confrontation. Most people want to avoid confrontation at all costs because it usually ends badly. I think we fail to see that the subsequent forgiveness following confrontation mirrors the forgiveness we have in Christ. We admire parents who consistently teach and discipline their children to behave properly. We admire teachers who bring out the best in their students, correcting their mistakes and providing solutions. We admire athletic coaches who push kids to excel and who correct their techniques and enhance their skills. We admire discipline and confrontation in many areas of our lives, so it's ironic that people in the church resist the concept of biblical confrontation. Gospel coaching seeks to protect the disciple by biblically confronting as often as needed to encourage healthy leaders and healthy churches.[9]

Accountability agreements can apply to any aspect of a person's life — personal, spiritual, or missional. For instance, an act of obedience may be losing ten pounds because a disciple is coming to see that their health is threatened by their weight. Another act of obedience may be paying off a credit card debt as a result of examining personal finances. Another response may be to develop a plan for organizing small groups within the church in response to the call of God to proclaim the gospel in various neighborhoods. The coach will review the accountability agreements to ensure the disciple keeps making progress as they produce fruit in keeping with repentance.

Using the phrase "accountability agreements" may sound a bit silly when the actual process of accountability is quite similar to the "action steps" we talked about earlier. But we intentionally separate these out. Since it is our aim to keep the gospel at the center of every decision that is made, calling these accountability responses or assignments "action steps" increases the tendency we have to make them one more legalistic box we tick off, devoid of gospel motivation. Done properly, a disciple will be continually reminded that *every* decision they make is in response to the gospel, that they are producing fruit in keeping with repentance, and are finding redemption in the finished work of Christ and not in modifying their behavior. Our inclination is to be our own savior by accomplishing our own will and with our own strength and wisdom for our own glory. We may wrongly believe that if we are disciplined enough to take steps of action to accomplish a goal, we will succeed. But the gospel calls us to lay down our strength, our wisdom, and our will at the foot of the cross (bowing to the finished work of Jesus). We do not possess the ability to accomplish anything except through the Spirit of God, who calls us to repentance. The subsequent fruit of this repentance is expressed by obedience through Christ who alone strengthens us (Philippians 4:13).

In the next chapter, we pull all of this together and discuss what a sample coaching session looks like.

CHAPTER 13

PUTTING IT ALL TOGETHER

RECENTLY, I INTERVIEWED CHRIS SCOTT, MD, a dermatologist in Charlottesville, Virginia, and a visiting lecturer at the University of Virginia, to ask him to describe a visit to a doctor's office from the perspective of a physician. He said the office visit begins with his knock on the door and the patient's invitation into the examination room. Dr. Scott went on to say that he engages in conversation to put the patient at ease and to build trust in his role as the health provider, connecting with his patient relationally. Then he asks about the regimen prescribed in past visits and how successful the treatments have been, reviewing the past history. But Dr. Scott said that the most important aspect of the visit is *identifying the chief concern* of the patient. This is the issue that is most urgent, the one causing the most pain, or the one that has risen to the top as the most critical need. In other words, they look to discover the *objective* of their time together.

The chief concern or objective must be identified early, or else the time spent together may be relationally wonderful but of little benefit to the other person's physical health. Dr. Scott examines the patient carefully to discern their chief concern. Forty percent of the time, Dr. Scott reports that he finds a lesion or suspicious mole that the patient doesn't even know existed. His patients give him permission to examine them for other health-threatening problems as well. Once the chief concern is identified, Dr. Scott begins exploring medical options to address the concern. Finally, Dr. Scott either affirms the treatment regimen or prescribes a new treatment to bring health to the patient.

Much like a doctor, a gospel coach *connects* relationally with his disciple (*C* - Connect), and spends time *reviewing* past sessions and any agreed-on regimens or accountability (*R* - Review). Much of the coaching session is spent focusing on particular *objectives* and goals that have been decided on for the session based on the chief concerns (*O* - Objectives). A coach examines, probes, and investigates the disciple for areas in their life that are not lined up with the gospel, and like surgical intervention, this probing is an expression of love and care for the other person to address problem areas in order to bring health to their lives (*S* - Strategies). Finally, a gospel coach must recognize that all that is done in their time together is dependent on Spirit empowerment and intervention petitioned through prayer (*S* - Supplication and Spirit).

The most effective form of gospel coaching takes place when people intentionally engage in conversations that honor the clearly defined and distinct roles of coach and disciple. Mark Driscoll and I have regular casual conversations in the office, at events, and in meetings. But our intentional coaching sessions are our most productive time together. During these times we take notes and have specific accountability and do pastoral care, confession, repentance, and mutual equipping for the calling of God to make disciples, plant churches, and train people.

BEFORE THE SESSION

There are several keys to having a fruitful coaching session that can be addressed prior to meeting together. The time you invest as a coach before the session is key to getting the most out of your limited time with the disciple.

TAKE THE TIME TO PREPARE

Block out at least fifteen minutes before the session to think and pray through the session. Keep your Bible close at hand so that you can speak scriptural truth into the life of the disciple. Another element of preparation is to pay attention to your own (as a coach) personal walk with the Lord. Take time to refresh your understanding of the gospel in your own life, saturating your mind with Scripture and allowing the Spirit to fill you anew. Otherwise, you may be tempted to depend on your own wisdom. Thankfully, the power of the Holy Spirit is not dependent on the coach's relationship with God, and the Spirit will work in spite of a gospel coach's sin and frailty. However, a coach should still seek to truthfully model what they are asking of the disciple, and this requires them to be continually abiding in Christ. The coach who is abiding in Christ will find that frequently what they are learning from Jesus will directly translate into the life situation of their disciple and ignite incredible Holy Spirit-directed breakthrough and growth for the disciple. There is amazing power in a coach passing on what is fresh in their heart about the gospel.

Mentally Map Your Conversation

You are not going to be able to cover every need of the disciple in a single session, or entirely develop a disciple's calling, goals, steps of action, and stewardship in an hour. But you can map where you intend to go in a session, and there can be logical progression. Using the CROSS method, you will likely need to focus on two to three areas. You may need to limit your focus to just *connecting* and *reviewing*, especially in the early stages of a coaching relationship. At other times, you may spend five minutes of your session *connecting* and then devote the rest of the session to *objectives* and *strategies*. Try to focus your questions and discussion around the mental map you have laid out for the session (with the freedom, of course, to change directions if something big comes up).

One wise coach noted to me that if a session seems dead, rote, or lifeless, it may be helpful to go back to the previous step on the coaching journey. For instance, if you are working with a disciple on *strategies* and the brainstorming time proves fruitless, or the disciple seems to have no idea how to do anything he is supposed to do and never completes any of the accountability agreements, then at this point they could go back to the *objectives*. Additionally, when the disciple does not seem to be opening up or concerned about any-thing (everything is always "going all right"), this is an indicator that the coach and disciple have not connected well and established a solid relationship or enough trust. The coach needs to step back from *reviewing* and begin to *connect* once again. The coach may need to know the disciple better and revise the session to listen to the disciple rather than pushing them forward with a life plan.

With this in mind, let's look at what a coaching session might look like.

A SAMPLE SESSION
PREPARING FOR THE SESSION

It's Monday, and I have a coaching call scheduled with Johnny Leader on Thursday. I log on to the coaching website and review our session from two weeks ago. I notice that I had asked Johnny about challenges in his ministry as the volunteer youth pastor at his church, and he shared his discontent, noting that he wanted to quit his secular job and serve the church full-time. In the previous ses-sion, we discussed his perceived need for this role and his feeling that he was going through the motions because he didn't have enough time to invest in ministry. The heart of the issue, we determined, was Johnny's *identity* in his church position—he wanted a more secure role for himself rather than truly serving Jesus in this capacity with joy. While Johnny had recognized this about himself, we did not have the time to get to a place in our conversation where he felt con-victed of his need for security.

I noticed that the last time we met, I began by asking him how his personal time with the Lord was going. He had responded that he hadn't read the Bible or prayed on his own for several weeks. We had reviewed his busy schedule, and I nudged him toward blocking out time and finding a place where he wouldn't be distracted—and we put that on his accountability agreement in our session.

So now I open a new session online and begin to enter ques-tions. The first is simple: "How did it go getting some time away to read your Bible and pray?" I want to know that he actually followed through with his plan, and I'm interested to see what the Holy Spirit did in that time. I post a few more questions about his frustrations with ministry to get an update, and then add other questions to gauge what irritations may have affected his life—his family dynamics, his sleep, his relationships, and his ministry to the students. After I complete the session questions, I send an e-mail to Johnny to let him know his session is ready. I ask him to respond to all the questions by Wednesday, which allows me a day to review his answers before our session.

THE DAY OF THE SESSION

Just before the session begins, I review Johnny's answers to the questions I posted earlier in the week. I begin praying and asking God to reveal Johnny's heart to me and to show me how to shepherd him well. Johnny's answer to my question about his sleep strikes me. He is working seventy hours a week in his two jobs and typically sleeps five hours a night. He seems almost proud of this, and he has made a witty comment about how caffeine and sugar have become his best friends. What I perceive is that he is finding identity in his success and has an inability to rest in God. This is the issue I decide we need to discuss in our coaching session.

When I call him, I have his session in front of me online. After spending a few minutes connecting relationally, I have him pray for our time together, and then I begin exploring the issues. I first ask clarifying questions and listen, silently praying for the Holy Spirit to bring illumination and give me wisdom. For my later reference, I type private notes into the session (with a feature designed for this) that Johnny can't see. When I sense the Spirit prompting me to speak up, I start telling Johnny the good news—that Jesus' work is the work that counts, that Johnny has nothing to offer, that God is not demanding anything more from him, that resting in Christ is receiving God's grace and acknowledging that God works and that God saves.

A minor breakthrough occurs when Johnny realizes he needs to change his schedule to fulfill his calling to love his family and to serve his church—but ultimately to fulfill his calling to live as a child of God first. I ask him questions concerning the responsibilities he can reasonably eliminate or delegate. I ask him who is consuming most of his time and how he may be able to incorporate physical exercise and adequate sleep. I ask him what it looks like to lovingly pursue his wife and children. I challenge Johnny to evaluate his schedule and realign it as a good steward with his calling and with his need to worship God and rest in him. We post this task to his accountability agreement section as an item to review during our next session.

Finally, we pray together about our desire to glorify God through our frail lives and to respond to the Holy Spirit's convicting and empowering ministry. We both pray and then thank each other for the time we spent together. After confirming the time and date of our next session, I end in the same way I always do — by affirming God's transforming work in his life. After a grueling session, I want the disciple to be reminded that "he [God] who began a good work in you will bring it to completion at the day of Jesus Christ" (Philippians 1:6).

PREPARING FOR THE NEXT SESSION

I typically spend ten to fifteen minutes examining the session while it is fresh in my mind, and I begin creating a new coaching session. I ask questions that will build on this session, as well as a general question that allows Johnny to address any other pressing challenges he is facing. I also take note of anything that I promised to provide him with, whether it is information or feedback. I can upload any pertinent documents on the Internet-based coaching environment or simply e-mail it to him. I finish with a prayer for him and the challenges he is facing.

CONCLUSION

As you can see, a coaching session is not complicated, nor is every session identical. Coaching with the gospel relies, most importantly, on the gospel itself. As mentioned earlier in this book, most coaching for church leaders is primarily focused on methodology. We believe that methods are important, just as maps are necessary when traveling, but methods are not value neutral. They take you places. They have consequences. In some respects, the typical performance-centered approach to coaching is too shortsighted. It focuses on temporary goals for this life, goals that may not have an eternal impact. If the desire is to lead a church that is centered on the gospel of Jesus Christ, the approach to coaching leaders in the development of the church should also have a gospel centrality, a focus that leads to an eternal impact.

Effective coaching is about friendship, but it is a unique type of friendship built on a mutual commitment to the gospel. A method of coaching that bypasses the gospel friendship may, in the long term, fail to assist leaders in making progress in a personal lifestyle and in the health of the church they serve. Dick Kaufmann noted that the most desperate need for believers "is to hear and appropriate the gospel to their lives," for the gospel empowers us for service. It "gives us a whole new motivational structure" and "sets us free to love and serve unconditionally in response to God's grace in Christ."[1] The grace of God found in the gospel story invites us to become vulnerable with others with whom we have a relationship. Without Christ, we have a natural aversion to vulnerability, to "being known." But a coaching friendship, grounded in trust and grace, can be a powerful tool for equipping every ministry leader in the church.

Every church leader needs to be coached with a gospel-centered approach to produce healthy, reproductive communities of believers. Every church leader needs to be coaching other leaders to make disciples who are identifying with Christ, worshiping God passionately, uniting with a community, and missionally engaging with people of all nations. Churches that desire to be rich in bearing godly fruit that blesses their city, their relationships with one another, their communication and worship, and their service will benefit by having their leaders being coached by gospel-centered leaders.

Coaching is an intentional gospel conversation among friends, with focused discussions about a disciple's personal, spiritual, and missional life. Have fun as you are transformed for God's glory.

> We all, with unveiled face, beholding the glory of the Lord, are being transformed into the same image from one degree of glory to another. For this comes from the Lord who is the Spirit.
> —*2 Corinthians 3:18*

RESOURCES

INTERNET RESOURCE

To facilitate the organization and process of gospel coaching, we created a website as a tool to enable the coach to shepherd the disciple more efficiently. Gospel coaching and its principles do not require using the website. Even if the Internet is not available, we believe that the principles outlined in this book can still be implemented effectively. However, we have found that using a web-based tool greatly facilitates coaching in six ways:

1. It facilitates a practical forum for knowing, feeding, leading, and protecting the disciple.
2. It helps the coach to organize and track the disciple's progress.
3. It accelerates and focuses the sessions.
4. It monitors accountability agreements.
5. It provides a repository for shared documents.
6. It provides a calendar to make appointments.

Internet-based dialogues in which the disciple submits answers to the coach's questions prior to the coaching session concentrate the conversation toward the most pressing and important needs of the disciple. Sending questions a few days before the meeting allows the disciple more time to think through and prayerfully respond to the questions.

It also allows the coach to review the answers in advance, pray through issues raised, and focus the conversation with the disciple. The disciple and the coach can enter additional information into the online forum to record thoughts, ideas, problems, and progress as the coaching session is taking place.

A commonly cited objection to using the Internet for discipleship is that it seems phony or nonrelational. On the contrary, we have found that the web tool promotes deep relationships. Much of the supportive information is provided by the dialogue exchange online. The coach is able to hear thoughts from the disciple ahead of time; then in their live conversation, the coach can devote more attention to the heart of the disciple. Without this prior dialogue, the coach may need to spend a significant portion of their time together gathering information about the disciple before being able to determine the objective of the coaching session.

If you are interested in training in this Internet-based coaching resource, visit www.GospelCoach.com for more details.

GOSPEL COACH CERTIFICATION

In addition, while one can be a coach without having gone through a formal certification process, we encourage those who wish to become proficient in this model to pursue training that enhances competence in the ten gospel coach qualities:

1. relating personally
2. nourishing with truth
3. inspiring toward Jesus
4. equipping in needs
5. investing sacrificially
6. overseeing every aspect of a person's life
7. guiding with Spirit-empowered discernment
8. displaying compassion
9. comforting with hope in the gospel
10. fighting for their good

The certification process involves reading this book, *Gospel Coach*, attending a gospel coach training certification, successfully completing the gospel coach assessment test, coaching two disciple-leaders for ten sessions each, demonstrating coaching competence measured by two disciples and a self-evaluation, and submitting a certification analysis portfolio. To get started or to find out additional information about this process, e-mail GospelCoach@gmail.com.

COACH AND DISCIPLE COVENANT

COVENANT TIME FRAME

- Specify start and end dates—at least six months.
- Note whether there will be the opportunity to continue the relationship and to clarify expectations by both parties; establish a time when a decision will be made whether or not to renew a covenant and continue meeting.

AGENDA AND GOALS

- To equip the disciple with the necessary training, support, discipleship, and mentoring to bring them to a place of effective leadership anchored in deep personal knowledge and experience of the gospel.
- To take six months to focus especially on the development of the disciple's personal, spiritual, and missional life.
- To see the coach leading the disciple by example in calling the disciple to personal repentance and reception of the gospel in their personal life, spiritual walk, and missional calling.
- Add any specific priorities here ...

MEETINGS

- The coach will initiate the scheduling of two monthly meetings of forty-five minutes each.
- The coach will send session questions and notes at least two days in advance of each meeting.
- The disciple will answer session questions and submit them to the coach at least one day prior to the session.
- Both the coach and disciple agree to make their meetings a priority and to be punctual for them.

ADDITIONAL CONTACT AND RELATIONSHIP

- If additional contact or relationship is requested or permissible, outline the nature of the relationship and its boundaries here ...

COMMITMENTS AND EXPECTATIONS

- *Biblical, gospel-centered coaching.* The foundation of all our teaching, advice, help, correction, and rebuke will be based in Scripture and in line with the gospel. We will not stray toward adopting secular methods that ignore or reject true wisdom. We will submit to the authority of Jesus and his Word in all matters in coaching.
- *Servanthood.* We commit to being servants of God, of one another, of those we coach, and of the church.
- *Honesty and vulnerability.* We will speak the truth in love. We will openly share that which the Holy Spirit prompts in us. We will openly share both life and ministry issues with those we coach. We refuse to practice cunning or deceit with one another.
- *Full engagement.* We commit to be people of our word; we will do what we say we will. We will take this relationship seriously, listening and taking to heart each conversation. Whenever something is clear or truly agreed on, we commit to work through it until there is full agreement and understanding rather than skimming the surface with superficial congeniality.

- *Confidentiality.* We will maintain trust and relationship by not sharing outside the congregations or individuals we have opportunity to coach.
- *Punctuality and preparedness.* We will be prompt for all appointments and phone calls out of respect for each other.
- *Ethics.* We will model the highest level of Christian character.
- *Prayer.* We will support one another in prayer throughout this relationship.

COVENANT COMMITMENTS

We commit ourselves to fulfilling the elements of this covenant. We commit to active partnership and support with all certified coaches within the guidelines above. As brothers in Christ, we strive to keep these commitments and ask for Jesus' perfect help, empowerment, and guidance through Scripture and the Holy Spirit.

Disciple's signature _____

     Date_____

Coach's signature _____

     Date_____

APPENDIX 2

INTAKE FORM

THIS FORM IS HELPFUL in establishing a gospel coach and disciple relationship. It facilitates the coach's getting to know the disciple and establishes a starting point for the journey toward Jesus and his calling in the disciple's life.

Feel free to revise this form to include only the questions that will be beneficial for your particular gospel coaching relationship. This list is quite comprehensive and is meant to be selectively utilized.

PERSONAL LIFE
Know

1. Tell me about your family [spouse, children's names and ages, etc.].
2. When is your birthday? Anniversary?
3. What makes you excited or feel really alive?
4. What are some skills and talents God has blessed you with?
5. What have been lifelong desires and dreams for you? What is going on with these dreams and desires now?
6. What are you hoping for in the next six months?
7. How has God saved you personally? How is he saving you daily?
8. How would you describe a "perfect day"?

9. How would you describe a "terrible day"?
10. How is ministry impacting your family?
11. How is your family impacting your ministry?
12. How is your ministry impacting your faith?
13. How is your faith impacting your ministry?
14. How is your personality affecting others?
15. How are others affecting your personality?
16. How is your integrity impacting others? What people are influencing your integrity both positively and negatively?
17. How is your character influencing your culture?
18. How is your character influencing your church community?
19. How are you developing character in your leaders?
20. How is your physical health?
    - What does your exercise look like weekly?
    - What do you do for recreation?
    - What does your eating look like daily?
    - What does your sleep and rest look like?
    - Do you have any health issues that affect your life and ministry? How are you dealing with these?
21. How is your emotional health?
    - How is ministry affecting your emotions?
    - How are your emotions affecting your ministry?
    - What tone are you setting in your home through your emotions?
    - What tone are you setting in your ministry through your emotions?

FEED

1. What area of your character in your personal life are you most convicted about by the Holy Spirit?
    - What do you envision this developed area to look like?
    - How would you describe this area now?
    - What things could you do to develop or grow in this area?
    - What commitment do you have to grow in this area?

- What has made it difficult for you to see growth or change in this area?
2. What is currently confusing you about the gospel on a heart level?
3. What books are you currently reading? What are you learning?
4. How can I encourage, help, and support you?
5. How are you making space to be refreshed in God's salvation in a personal, practical way?

LEAD

1. What is holding you back from personal growth in Jesus?
2. What are you holding on to that is keeping you from being more like Christ?
3. What current personal failures are most frustrating to you?
4. What has God accomplished in your character in the last year?
5. How has God shown his faithfulness to you in the last year?
6. How are you and God doing?
7. Where do you think God wants you to go in your personal growth in the next six months? Why?
8. What does it look like for you to listen to and be led by the Holy Spirit on a daily basis?

PROTECT

1. Who do you need to help you?
2. To whom will you be accountable?
3. How can I help you?
4. Where do we really need God to show up?
5. Where is your heart hard?
6. What lies do you believe?
7. What doubts have crept in?
8. In what ways have you invited unbelief and deception in your personal life? How can I help you close those doors?
9. How will we pray?

MINISTRY CALL

KNOW

1. How would you describe your personal call?
2. What people and circumstances are associated with your call to ministry?
3. How and when has your call to ministry been affirmed in your life?
4. How have others affirmed your call to ministry?
5. What opportunities do you have to fulfill this calling?

FEED

1. What leadership gifts or abilities do you need to develop to fulfill your calling or current assignment?
2. How would you describe your current abilities in this area?
3. What options do you have to develop your leadership?
4. What will you do to develop your leadership?

LEAD

1. When has your call to leadership been challenged?
2. Under what circumstances have you doubted your call?
3. Is there anything in this current experience that is causing you to question your call?
4. What activities or events do you use to anchor, firm up, or strengthen your call?
5. How should your call be focused or clarified?
6. What does your call's success look like?

PROTECT

1. Who have been the mentors in your life?
2. What mentors and coaches do you need now to fulfill your call?
3. Who else do you need to help you?
4. What do you need most from God right now?

SPIRITUAL LIFE

KNOW

1. What are some of the major milestones in your theological development?
2. What are you reading in Scripture right now? What are you learning about God?
3. How do you practice abiding in Jesus?
4. What increases your affections toward God and others?
5. What deadens your affections toward God and others?
6. What is causing you anxiety or fear right now?

FEED

1. What are some areas with which you wrestle theologically?
2. What information are you missing?
3. How hungry are you to know God?
4. How dependent do you feel on Jesus in your life?

LEAD

1. What discrepancies may be emerging between what your mind knows and what your heart believes in Scripture?
2. How is the Holy Spirit leading you to grow in your understanding of Jesus?
3. What does your prayer life look like?
4. Who are the people in your life you are praying for?
5. What are you praying for?
6. What are your prayers revealing about your faith?
7. Who is effectively bringing you clarity about who Jesus is and about the truth of Scripture? How are you prioritizing these people in your life?

PROTECT

1. What are you feeding yourself with to feel satisfied outside of Christ?
2. What current obstacles hinder your spiritual growth?

3. Who is pulling you away from your relationship with God? How?

4. Who is planting doubt and discouragement in your heart about Jesus?

5. What anti-Christian spiritual teaching are you tempted to believe? Why?

6. What are you allowing to take priority over your relationship with Jesus? Why?

7. What obedience has Jesus called you to that you have been ignoring or trying to escape?

MISSIONAL LIFE
KNOW

1. What opportunities for mission are present in your life?

2. Who are the lost people God has brought into your life? What does your relationship with these people look like?

3. What percentage of your time is spent with people who do not know Jesus?

4. What are your spiritual gifts?

5. Describe your current ministry and missional responsibilities.
   - Do these match your calling?
   - Are any of these activities being performed under compulsion?

6. To what degree do you and your church understand the prevailing culture in your city?

7. How do you and your church engage the culture?

8. How do you and your church serve the culture?

9. How and where do you and your church attract the culture?

10. How and where do you and your church initiate relationships in the culture?

11. How is your church perceived by the culture?

12. How do you and your church receive the culture?

13. How do your leaders impact the culture?

FEED

1. Where is ignorance in your mission or ministry killing you?
2. Are you experiencing any physical or emotional burnout?
   - How easily discouraged are you in your mission?
   - How passionate are you about your mission?
   - How is your patience quotient? Are you easily angered in your ministry?
   - Are you disconnecting completely from your mission for Sabbath? How?
3. Which Christian missiologists have influenced and shaped your mission through their writing or preaching?
4. How would you like to see your church connect with the culture?
5. What can you personally do to connect with culture?
6. What is working now in connecting with culture?
7. What other possibilities do you see for you or your fellowship to connect with culture?

LEAD

1. What does success in your mission look like?
2. How will you know when you are accomplishing what God has called you to?
3. How close are you to that success now?
4. What roadblocks are you experiencing in accomplishing your mission?
5. Is the direction you are headed the direction to which you've been called?
6. Where and how have you and your church been effective at reaching into your culture?
7. Which of your leaders most impact the culture?
8. Who are the persons of peace with whom you are connecting?
9. Where has there been a significant network of evangelistic relationships?
10. What is stopping you or your church from engaging or impacting culture?

11. What one or two things could you and your church do to understand, engage, or receive your culture?

PROTECT

1. What is draining your energy and sapping life from you in your mission?
2. Who is attacking your mission—intentionally or unintentionally?
3. What voices of discouragement are you listening to?
4. What personal sins are hindering your mission and calling?
5. Where are you allowing cowardice to hinder your mission and leadership?
6. Where are you charging ahead of the Holy Spirit in your own strength?
7. Who has sinned against you, and how is it affecting the mission?
8. Who have you sinned against, and how have you dealt with it?
9. What keeps rising up to distract you and your people from the mission?
10. What risks are you willing to take to demonstrate dependence on God?
11. Who can help you understand your culture?
12. Where do you most need God's help?
13. How are you praying for needs in the culture?

FORTY LEADERSHIP ACCOUNTABILITY QUESTIONS

THE FOLLOWING QUESTIONS can be used to protect a disciple in his leadership skills and development. Each section can take up to one hour to discuss between a coach and a disciple.

SELF LEADERSHIP

1. How are you unique? (calling, gifts, passions, personality, experiences, sin patterns)
2. How do you stay inspired? How often do you practice this?
3. How do you apply the gospel to yourself? What is the message in your mind?
4. What are the rhythms of grace in your life? (Scripture, worship, prayer, community, family, time off)
5. What idols compete for your worship? How do you forsake each idol?
6. What sinful mental images repeatedly play in your head? How do you take those thoughts captive?

7. How are you stewarding the gifts you have for the greatest benefit? (time, resources, skills)

INTERPERSONAL LEADERSHIP

1. Who understands you best? Other than your family, who are the people with whom you share life together? (2 Timothy 2:2)
2. Whom do you pray for? What specific petitions are you praying for them?
3. Who would you like to choose to become one of your influencer friends? What is your plan for making this happen?
4. How are you telling "the truth in love" to the people under your leadership? When do you tend to "spin" something?
5. How faithful are you in being on time and following through with promises?
6. Do you say yes and no with clarity so that it builds confidence and trust?
7. Whom are the people you tend to try to please and why?
8. How are you discipling each of your children and your spouse? (if applicable)
9. Who really knows you?
10. What relationships are broken in your life? What are you doing to bring reconciliation?

ORGANIZATIONAL LEADERSHIP

1. How has God called you to serve him? How are you fulfilling this calling?
2. What things nudge you away from following your calling?
3. What is the most pressing leadership issue you are currently facing?
4. Do people in your leadership area know with clarity what you expect of them?
5. What are you doing well in your leadership? What needs your attention?
6. How do you encourage those you are leading to follow the objectives of your organization?

7. In what ways do you personify your calling?
8. What opportunities did you decline for the sake of fulfilling your objectives?
9. What are the stories that define the culture of your leadership area? How do you capture these stories? How are the stories being shared?

TEAM LEADERSHIP

1. Who is your team? (roles, styles)
2. Who is going to replace you?
3. How do you demonstrate your love for each team member?
4. What dysfunctions in your team are you addressing?
5. With whom do you sense the most synergy? How can you maximize this?
6. With whom do you sense the least synergy? Why? How are you minimizing this?
7. Whom do you struggle to trust? Why? How do you address issues of distrust with them?
8. What inspires each team member? (Ask each one, "What aspect of your work brings you the most joy, and what stories do you tend to tell most often?)
9. How do you empower your team members to exercise their greatest gifts and talents on the team?

PASTORAL LEADERSHIP

1. What does faithfulness in your calling look like for you?
2. In which young leaders are you investing your life to develop?
3. How are you making disciples?
4. How are you equipping others to serve Jesus' church more effectively?
5. How are you living in a missional way?

COACHING QUESTIONS

QUESTIONS FOR *KNOWING* YOUR DISCIPLE

PERSONAL

1. What are some evidences of grace in your life recently?
2. What can you tell me about your spouse and family?
3. How do you relax or what do you do for fun?
4. How is your spouse doing?
5. How are you doing as a couple?
6. Are there any new strains on your relationship that surprised you?
7. Has your spouse complained about your time together recently?

SPIRITUAL

1. How is the condition of your soul?
2. How would you describe your call to follow Jesus Christ?
3. What are some of the Christian communities you participate in and how do they encourage your walk with Jesus?
4. What is God doing in your heart right now?
5. How have you seen the Holy Spirit produce new fruit in your life?

Missional

1. What opportunities for ministry do you see before you?
2. What is God calling you to be or do?
3. What skills or abilities has God given you that help clarify your calling?

QUESTIONS FOR *FEEDING* YOUR DISCIPLE

Personal

1. What is God teaching you about your role as a husband and father/wife and mother?
2. What obstacles are you experiencing in your personal life?
3. How is your health? Are you taking any medications?
4. What would enhance your relationship with your spouse?

Spiritual

1. What information or resources would be helpful for your spiritual growth?
2. Where have you experienced the most spiritual growth lately?
3. What is the biggest threat to your oneness with Christ?
4. Where are you most vulnerable to sin?
5. What sins are you battling?
6. What compels you to worship God?

Missional

1. When have you had a significant impact on another person?
2. In what ways are you making disciples?
3. What are some challenges you are facing in your primary ministry responsibility?
4. What resources do you need to accomplish your ministry goals?

QUESTIONS FOR *LEADING* YOUR DISCIPLE

Personal

1. How are you leading your family?
2. What is the greatest need in your personal life? (Look for idols, agendas, identity struggles, and selfishness.)

SPIRITUAL

1. How is the Lord leading you to respond to him?
2. What is the greatest need in your spiritual life? (Look for idols, agendas, identity struggles, and selfishness.)

MISSIONAL

1. What is the Lord leading you to [pick one] know (head), feel (heart), or do (hands) with regard to ministry?
2. What is the mission of your ministry?
3. What is the greatest need in your ministry life?

QUESTIONS FOR *PROTECTING* YOUR DISCIPLE

PERSONAL

1. What challenges do you face personally?
2. What temptations occur in your personal life?
3. Where are you prone to wander personally? (health, finances, time, marriage, etc.)

SPIRITUAL

1. What challenges do you face spiritually?
2. What temptations occur in your spiritual life?
3. What kind of priority do you give to Bible reading and prayer in your life?
4. Where are you prone to wander spiritually?

MISSIONAL

1. What challenges do you face missionally?
2. What temptations occur in your ministry life?
3. Where are you prone to wander in ministry?

SEVEN-DAY PRAYER GUIDE

Reminder Row	SUNDAY	MONDAY	TUESDAY
Pattern for request	Our Father in heaven	*Our Father*, holy is your name	*Our Father*, your kingdom come
Priority for request	Sonship	Worship	Evangelism
Prayers for **Passions** of my heart (heart affections)			
Key **Person**			
Prayers for other **People**			
Pressing urgent requests			
Praise for answers to my prayers			

We suggest assigning each disciple-leader to this prayer project that uses the Lord's Prayer as a foundation for praying.

WEDNESDAY	THURSDAY	FRIDAY	SATURDAY
Our Father, your will be done on earth as it is in heaven	*Our Father*, give us this day our daily bread	*Our Father*, forgive us our debts as we forgive our debtors	*Our Father*, lead us not into temptation but deliver us from evil
Mercy	Generosity Contentment	Unity Reconciliation	Warfare

Taken from John Smed, *Seven Days of Prayer with Jesus* (Vancouver, B. C.: Grace Vancouver Church, 2006). Permisssion is granted to copy and distribute this tool for personal use and educational purposes. For an electronic version, e-mail info@prayercurrent.com.

FIRST FOUR COACHING SESSIONS: SAMPLES

PRE-SESSION GUIDE: INSTRUCTIONS FOR GETTING STARTED AND FOR SESSIONS 1 TO 4

Scheduling: You need to schedule two forty-five-minute calls per month. Schedule four to six appointments in advance.

Before Session 1: Review your coaching guides for Sessions 1 to 4. Set up your four calls with your disciple and send the instructions below.

Website: Let your disciple know where you will be communicating and conducting coaching sessions. The Gospel Coach website (www. GospelCoach.com) will allow an interface for coaching sessions as well as for making the coaching covenant an automatic form. Post the first session online or submit questions.

Letter: Here is a sample first letter to be sent to your disciple:

Dear _____,

Welcome to gospel coaching! To get started, we will schedule four to six coaching sessions for the next three months. I will call you so we can schedule these. I also need you to take a test, answer some questions so that I can get to know you, and fill out and return the coaching covenant.

At least two days prior to our first session, please send back to me the following:

- answers to the questions on the website (or in the attached document).
- your DiSC profile results; if available, upload the pdf of your score into the session
- coaching covenant (signed, unless you have questions); typing your name in as signature is sufficient

I look forward to connecting with you very soon!

Warmly,

GOSPEL COACH'S GUIDE: SESSION 1

Objectives. This session's objectives are as follows: (1) get to know the disciple, (2) establish a relationship and expectations, and (3) build trust.

Tools. You will need these tools: phone or Skype connection, session 1 questions, coach's guide for session 1, coaching covenant form, and DiSC results from disciple.

Philosophical instructions. Here are some helpful instructions:

1. This first session will establish much of the disciple's expectations for the remainder of the relationship. You need to clearly communicate your objectives to help them grow in:
   - gospel identity
   - gospel worship
   - gospel community
   - gospel mission
2. The first two calls with your disciple will entail a lot of information gathering to get to know them personally, spiritually, and missionally. As the gospel coach, you should spend very little time talking in these initial sessions except to outline the logistics of the relationship (five to ten minutes max).

3. Learn about them personally and store that information in an accessible place so you can get at it when you need it (spouse's name, kids' names and ages, hobbies, etc). If you are using the Gospel Coach website (www.GospelCoach.com), I like to use the floating box on the right. This is viewable only by the coach.

4. Trust is a prerequisite for a disciple to open up and receive correction and affirmation well. In your first sessions, do not focus on challenging what you think is wrong with the disciple or finding solutions that will fix their stated problems. Instead, establish the facts that you are listening, you care, and you are coming alongside the disciple to see Jesus formed more clearly in them.

5. Knowing is a prerequisite to accurate judgment. Some things may look clear on the surface, but don't draw settled conclusions about what you think "the issues" are in the disciple's life based on the first sessions. Keep asking questions and gathering information.

6. Your disciple should have taken the DiSC test before this session. If not, they'll need to take it before your second session. You should know your own DiSC profile as well (take the test if you haven't yet done so); look for ways in which you differ from your disciple, and be prepared to adapt your style of communication for them. For example, if you are a high D or I on the DiSC, you'll likely want to cover a large number of questions and skip over content that seems uninteresting. If your disciple is a high S or C, this approach may frustrate them and they may prefer to cover four to five questions in depth and want to go over everything. Be aware, and as the gospel coach, adapt your style to the needs of the disciple.

7. Take notes during this session. You are studying your disciple to know him uniquely. Look for answers to these questions: What makes them tick? How is God shaping them? Where have they come from? What are their unique experiences, skills, and dreams?

8. Make sure you cover a few logistics. Establish who will call whom, what canceling policies should apply, and whether the disciple may contact you outside the coaching call times (and in what ways).

Session instructions. Here are instructions for this session:

1. At least two days prior to the session, send your disciple the session 1 questions and the coaching covenant document. Make sure you personalize the note to your disciple in the "questions" section.
2. Advise your disciple (1) who will call whom; (2) what phone number or Skype address to use; (3) to answer all session questions at least one day prior to the session; and (4) to review the coaching covenant and send it back electronically signed (type name on the sign line and e-mail back) if there are no questions.
3. Prior to the session, read and then pray through the answers you received from your disciple. Ask the Holy Spirit to reveal to you where to ask more questions and dig deeper.
4. During the session, carry out the following:
   • Start on time and end on time.
   • Offer an opening prayer.
   • Review the coaching covenant together.
   • Review the DiSC test results.
   • Spend forty-five minutes listening and asking questions about the disciple's story, probing deeper into the questions answered ["tell me more" and "what else?"].
   • Offer a closing prayer.

SAMPLE QUESTIONS FOR SESSION 1

[Coach, make this personal] Hello. I'm excited to get to know you over the next six months. To get started, please answer the questions and return to me at least one day prior to our session. Thank you.

1. What can you tell me about yourself? (your family, your community, what your growing-up years were like, etc.)

2. How did you become a Christian? When is your birthday? Anniversary?

3. What are some good things God has done in your life recently?

4. What have been some recent major "aha" moments in your spiritual walk?

5. How do you relax or what do you do for fun?

6. On a scale of 1 to 10 (1 = lowest), how would you rate your physical health?

7. How would you rate your spiritual health?

8. How would you rate your emotional health?

9. How would you rate your marital health?

10. What did you learn about yourself from the DiSC test? (Let's review your results together.) Was anything surprising? Anything you disagree with in the assessment?

11. What is your current role(s) in ministry? In what ways are you involved in ministry?

12. What is your missional involvement? How are you proclaiming the good news to those who don't know Jesus?

13. What are three issues you are facing in your life right now?

14. What are some hopes you have for this coaching relationship?

15. How do you see me coming alongside you to support you?

16. Do you have any questions about the coaching covenant?

17. What can I pray about for you?

GOSPEL COACH'S GUIDE: SESSION 2

Objectives. This session's objectives are as follows: (1) continue to get to know the disciple, (2) establish a relationship, and (3) build trust.

Tools. You will need these tools: phone or Skype, session 2 questions, coach's guide for session 2.

Philosophical instructions. Here are some helpful instructions.

1. Review session 1's philosophical instructions.

2. Continue to get to know your disciple. This session digs

a little deeper into the disciple's current location on their journey toward Christ.

3. The next session will focus more narrowly on the disciple's calling.

Session instructions: Here are instructions for this session.

1. At least two days prior to the session, send or post the session 2 questions and the coaching covenant document. Make sure you personalize the questions for your disciple.
2. Remind your disciple to (1) answer all session questions at least one day prior to the session and (2) review the coaching covenant and send it back electronically signed (type name on the sign line and e-mail back) if they haven't done so yet.
3. Prior to the session, read and then pray through the answers you received from your disciple. Ask the Holy Spirit to reveal to you where to ask more questions and dig deeper.
4. During the session, carry out the following:
   • Start on time and end on time.
   • Connect relationally. (Don't skip this.)
   • Connect to the Holy Spirit and the gospel through prayer.
   • Review session 1 tasks (coaching covenant, questions answered, any new challenges that have emerged since the last session.
   • Offer a closing prayer.

SAMPLE QUESTIONS FOR SESSION 2

1. How are you doing? What are some ways God has blessed you recently? (Coach, add a personal question here based on the previous session.)
2. (Coach, add another follow-up question from the previous session.)
3. How is your family? (Coach, make this specific.)
4. Tell me about your current mission:
   • What new opportunities for mission are present in your life?

- To what degree do you and your church understand the prevailing culture in your city?
- How do you and your church engage the culture?
5. Tell me about your spiritual life:
- What compels you to worship God?
- How is God saving you daily?
6. Tell me more about your personal life:
- What are some goals you have in your personal life?
- How would you describe a "perfect day"?
- How would you describe a "perfect week"?
- What does your exercise look like weekly? What do your sleep and rest look like? How would you like to improve your eating habits?
- Do you have any health issues that affect your life and ministry? How are you dealing with these?
7. Is there anything else on your mind that you'd like to discuss?
8. How can I be praying for you?

GOSPEL COACH'S GUIDE: SESSION 3

Objectives. This session's objectives are as follows: (1) dig into the disciple's calling to bring clarity to how God has generally and specifically called the disciple and (2) gauge the disciple's level of awareness and understanding of God's call on their life.

Tools. You will need these tools: phone or Skype connection, session 3 questions, and coach's guide for session 3.

Philosophical instructions. Here are some helpful instructions:

1. You are still "pregame" in coaching. You are still establishing where the disciple is in terms of understanding and following their calling.
2. If your disciple seems lost with regard to what their calling is, this will likely be the focus of the majority of your relationship from this point forward.
3. Calling will determine objectives; objectives will determine steps of action; steps of action will determine steward-

ship (time, relationships, resources, etc). It is imperative to understand the disciple's calling prior to coaching them, as all issues will be focused under the lens of that calling. Other issues that seem to be "the problem" will fall away if they are not within the scope of the calling.

4. Read the section in chapter 11 of *Gospel Coach* titled "Working through a Gospel Life Plan" (if you haven't done so already).

5. The "spiritual life" and "personal life" questions in this session should help shed light on whether the disciple is actively seeking guidance from God (clarifying the calling) and whether the disciple has applied that calling in personal and ministry life (look for tension).

6. While we place a high value on the coach's leadership through the coaching relationship, ultimately the Holy Spirit leads the entire session. Remind yourself constantly to listen to the Holy Spirit, and ask for his help in knowing when to ask more questions and when to spark answers. There will be times for both, but don't underestimate the power of a good question to open the door to the Holy Spirit's work on the disciple's heart (think of how Jesus often taught his own disciples by asking questions to probe their hearts for gospel transformation).

Session instructions. Here are instructions for this session:

1. At least two days prior to the session, send or post the session 3 questions. Make sure you personalize the questions for your disciple.

2. Remind your disciple to answer all session questions at least one day prior to the session.

3. Prior to the session, read and then pray through the answers you received from your disciple. Ask the Holy Spirit to reveal to you where to ask more questions and dig deeper.

4. Don't forget to open and close the session by praying with and for the disciple.

Sample Questions for Session 3

1. How are you doing? What are some challenges you are facing? How's … (Coach, add a personal question here based on previous session.)
2. (Coach, add another follow-up question from previous session.)
3. How is your family? (Coach, make this specific.)
4. How has God called you personally, and to what?
   • What are some lifelong dreams you've had? What is going on with these dreams right now?
   • What skills or talents has God given you?
   • What makes you really excited and energetic for life? How much of this excitement is in your life now?
   • When have you had a significant impact on another person recently?
   • Where has God called you to be a light to those who don't know him? What does this look like in your life right now?
   • What would success look like in your calling?
5. Can you tell me more about your spiritual life?
   • What have you been reading in your Bible this week? What have you been learning from your reading?
   • How are you feeding your soul?
6. Can you tell me more about your personal life?
   • How is ministry affecting your family, friendships, and community?
   • How are your family, friends, and community affecting your ministry?
   • What helps you grow and develop personally? (your mind, your heart, your creativity, your skills, etc.) How do you foster personal growth in your life?
7. How can I be praying for you?

GOSPEL COACH'S GUIDE: SESSION 4

Objectives. This session's objectives are as follows: (1) continue to dig into the disciple's calling and (2) dig personally into their heart.

Tools. You will need these tools: phone or Skype connection, session 4 questions, and coach's guide for session 4.

Philosophical instructions. Here are some helpful instructions.

1. You should be customizing the session questions based on the knowledge you have gathered. Continue to add information to help you know the disciple better, but start focusing your questions further on their calling and heart's condition.

2. Be aware that in our culture (Christian and otherwise), we don't commonly address arrogance, despair, or apathy in our hearts. Most of us will not offer this information to others unless specifically asked. However, not only are these characteristics indicators of deep heart issues and disbelief; they are serious impediments to hearing and fulfilling a call from God.

3. Look for disconnects between what the disciple says they believe and how they actually live.

Session instructions. Here are instructions for the session:

1. At least two days prior to the session, send or post the session 4 questions. Make sure you personalize the questions for your disciple.

2. A sample session has been provided. From here on out, you should be customizing questions. You can use the master list of questions to help you build sessions, but as you get to know your disciple better, with the Holy Spirit's prompting, strive to build your sessions to uniquely fit the disciple and spur them on to rooting their identity in Christ, worshiping God and not created things, being in true and deep community, and living out Christ's mission for the world through the church.

3. Remind your disciple to answer all session questions at least one day prior to the session.

4. Prior to the session, read and pray through the answers you received from your disciple. Ask the Holy Spirit to reveal to you where to ask more questions and dig deeper.

5. Don't forget to open and close the session by praying with and for the disciple.

SAMPLE QUESTIONS FOR SESSION 4

1. How are you doing? What good things are happening in your life?
2. (Make sure to add personal questions and follow-up questions from previous sessions.)
3. What leadership gifts or abilities do you need to develop to fulfill your calling?
   - How would you describe your current abilities in these areas?
   - How is God providing ways for you to become equipped in these areas?
   - What opportunities do you have to develop your leadership?
   - When has your call to leadership been challenged?
   - Under what circumstances have you doubted your call?
   - Is anything currently causing you to question your call?
4. How is your heart?
   - How would you rate your heart's tendency toward *despair*?
   - What causes you despair?
   - What alleviates your feelings of despair?
   - How would you rate your heart's tendency toward *arrogance*?
   - What inflames your arrogance?
   - How is arrogance manifested in your home?
   - How is arrogance manifested in your ministry and mission?
   - How is arrogance manifested in your spiritual life?
   - How would you rate your heart's tendency toward *apathy*?
   - What have seasons of apathy looked like for you?
   - What causes apathy in your heart?
   - Where is your heart now in terms of despair, arrogance, and apathy?
5. What are you praying about right now?

NOTES

Introduction

1. Paul D. Stanley and J. Robert Clinton, *Connecting: The Mentoring Relationships You Need to Succeed in Life* (Colorado Springs: NavPress, 1992), 47–85.

Chapter 1

1. "Coach (Carriage)," http://en.wikipedia.org/wiki/Coach_(carriage). The term *coach* was later applied to railway cars in 1866 (www.etymonline.com/index. php?term=coach).
2. See "coach (n)," www.etymonline.com/index.php?term=coach.
3. Patrick Williams and Deborah C. Davis, *Therapist as Life Coach: Transforming Your Practice* (New York: Norton, 2002), 29.
4. Paul D. Stanley and J. Robert Clinton, *Connecting: The Mentoring Relationships You Need to Succeed in Life* (Colorado Springs: NavPress, 1992), 18, 73.
5. Ed Stetzer and Phillip Connor, "Church Planting Survivability and Health Study," Center for Missional Research, North American Mission Board (February 2007).
6. Steve Ogne and Tim Roehl, *Transformissional Coaching* (Nashville: Broadman &Holman, 2008), 80.
7. Gary Collins, *Christian Coaching* (Colorado Springs: NavPress, 2001), 31.
8. See Archibald Hart, "Time To Get a Life," *Cutting Edge* (Spring 2001), 14–16.
9. Augustine, *Soliloquies*, 2.7.14; quoted in George Howie, *Educational Theory and Practice in St. Augustine* (London: Routledge, 1969), 170.
10. Gunter Krallman, *Mentoring for Mission: A Handbook on Leadership Principles Exemplified by Jesus Christ* (Waynesboro, Ga.: Gabriel, 2002), 63.
11. David Allen, *Getting Things Done: The Art of Stress-Free Productivity* (New York: Penguin, 2002).

Chapter 2

1. See Chris Armstrong, "Preacher in the Hands of an Angry Church," *Leadership Journal* 24 (Winter 2003), www.ctlibrary.com/le/2003/winter/8.52.html.
2. Paul Vitello, "Taking a Break from the Lord's Work," *New York Times*, August 1, 2010, A1, www.nytimes.com/2010/08/02/nyregion/02burnout.html?_r=4&pagewanted=1 (accessed August 9, 2010).
3. David Olson, *The American Church in Crisis* (Grand Rapids: Zondervan, 2008), 15, 30.
4. Christian Smith, "On 'Moralistic Therapeutic Deism' as U.S. Teenagers' Actual, Tacit, De Facto Religious Faith," www.ptsem.edu/uploadedFiles/School_of_Christian_Vocation_and_Mission/Institute_for_Youth_Ministry/Princeton_Lectures/Smith-Moralistic.pdf (accessed May 30, 2010).
5. Tim Keller, "The Centrality of the Gospel," www.redeemer2.com/resources/papers/centrality.pdf (accessed December 19, 2011).
6. "Pastors' Forum: How do you deal with stress in the ministry?" Tony Cooke Ministries, www.tonycooke.org/forum/answers/stress_ministry.html (accessed November 16, 2011).
7. Abraham Maslow, considered by many to be the father of humanistic psychology, was

largely responsible for injecting much credibility and energy into the human potential movement of the 1960s with the publication of his seminal treatise *Toward a Psychology of Being* (1968). In this work, Maslow summarized his research of "self-actualizing people" (a term first coined by Kurt Goldstein) and coined terms such as "full humanness" and wrote about "being" and "becoming." Maslow studied the "healthy personality" of people who he termed self-actualizers; he researched, questioned, and observed people who were living with a sense of vitality and purpose and who were constantly seeking to grow psychologically and achieve more of their human potential. It is this key point in history that we believe set the framework for the field of life coaching to emerge in the 1990s. Information taken from Patrick Williams and Deborah C. Davis, *Therapist as Life Coach: Transforming Your Practice* (New York: Norton, 2002), 13.

8. Carl Jung also believed in the power of connectedness and relationships, as well as a "future orientation" or teleological belief that we create our futures through visioning and purposeful living. Jung's theories and approaches also emphasized spirituality and values expressed as one goes through the process he called individuation—the progression and development of the spiritual self. Jung also described the importance of myths and rituals, which are increasingly becoming important components for clients of life coaches. Information taken from Williams and Davis, *Therapist as Life Coach*, 13.

9. Alfred Adler saw himself as a personal educator, believing that every person develops a unique life approach that shapes their goals, values, habits, and personal drives. He believed that happiness arises from a sense of significance and social connectedness (belonging), not merely individual objectives and desires. Adler saw each person as the creator and artist of their life and frequently involved his clients in goal setting, life planning, and inventing their future—all tenets and approaches in life coaching today. Information taken from Williams and Davis, *Therapist as Life Coach*, 14.

10. Milton Erickson, an iconoclastic and unique psychiatrist, believed in the inherent ability of individuals to achieve wellness if the reason for an illness could be thwarted. Erickson often achieved seemingly "miraculous results" from just a few sessions with a patient. Information taken from Williams and Davis, *Therapist as Life Coach*, 13.

11. "People with problems in living" is a rubric coined by Thomas Szasz to replace the term "mental illness." It can be used to describe the problems caused by addictions, substance abuse, antisocial behavior, and a multitude of degrading labels.

12. The full realization of one's potential. See Abraham H. Maslow, *Motivation and Personality*, 3rd ed. (New York: Harper, 1987).

13. Larry Crabb, *Basic Principles of Christian Counseling* (Grand Rapids: Zondervan, 1975), 32–33.

14. The CCT approach has roots in Freudian thinking, according to Rogers. See also Carl R. Rogers, "Significant Aspects of Client-Centered Therapy," *American Psychologist* 1 (1946), 415–22, http://psychclassics.yorku.ca/Rogers/therapy.htm (accessed November 16, 2011).

15. For example, John Whitmore's GROW approach utilized by several godly Christian leaders.

16. John Whitmore, *Coaching for Performance: GROWing Human Potential and Purpose*, 4th ed. (London: Brealey, 2009), 13.

17. Jane Creswell, *Christ-Centered Coaching* (St. Louis, Mo.: Lake Hickory Resources, 2006), 13.

18. David Powlison, "Idols of the Heart and 'Vanity Fair,'" *Journal of Biblical Counseling*, 13, no. 2 (Winter 1995): 35.

19. Henri Nouwen, *In the Name of Jesus* (New York: Crossroad, 1993), 65–66.

20. J. I. Packer, *Evangelism and the Sovereignty of God* (Downers Grove, Ill.: InterVarsity, 1991), 55.

21. "The Story: How It All Began and How It Will Never End," Spread Truth Ministries (2010), http://viewthestory.com/3156.

22. Martin Luther, *Commentary on Galatians*, trans. Theodore Graebner (Grand Rapids: Zondervan, 1949), Gal. 4:6.

23. C. S. Lewis, *God in the Dock: Essays on Theology and Ethics* (Grand Rapids: Eerdmans, 1970), 87.
24. "The Story: How It All Began and How It Will Never End," http://viewthestory.com/3156.
25. Steve Childers, "True Spirituality: The Transforming Power of the Gospel," www.gca.cc/other_files/True%20Spirituality%20by%20Childers.pdf (accessed March 7, 2011).
26. Robert Heppe, "The Gospel, Sanctification, and Mission" (unpublished paper).
27. C. S. Lewis, *The Last Battle* (New York: HarperCollins, 1994), 172.
28. Richard P. Kaufmann, "The Gospel-Driven Church" (unpublished lecture notes), based on Harbor Presbyterian's core value #1.

CHAPTER 3

1. Matthew 11:28–29; 28:18; Philippians 3:8–9, 12; John 15:2–12; Romans 7:18; 1 John 2:27; 1 Corinthians 1:30; Galatians 2:20; 2 Corinthians 1:21; 6:2.
2. John Calvin, *Institutes of the Christian Religion*, ed. John T. McNeill (Philadelphia: Westminster, 1960), 1:108; John Calvin, *Commentary on Acts*, vol. 2 (Grand Rapids: Christian Classics Ethereal Library, 1999), 234.
3. See Os Guinness and John Seel, *No God But God* (Chicago: Moody, 1992).

CHAPTER 4

1. J.I. Packer, *Knowing God* (Downers Grove, Ill.: InterVarsity, 1993), 188.
2. Steve Brown, *When Being Good Isn't Good Enough* (Grand Rapids: Baker, 1995), 143.
3. Timothy Keller, *The Reason for God* (New York: Penguin, 2008), 171.
4. Mark Driscoll, "Resisting Idols Like Jesus," www.marshillchurch.org/media/1st-corinthians/resisting-idols-like-jesus (accessed July 30, 2010).
5. Quoted in Timothy Keller, *Gospel in Life Study Guide: Grace Changes Everything* (Grand Rapids: Zondervan, 2010), 28.
6. Richard F. Lovelace, *Dynamics of Spiritual Life: An Evangelical Theology of Renewal* (Downers Grove, Ill.: InterVarsity, 1979), 90.
7. Thomas Watson, *The Doctrine of Repentance* (Carlisle, Pa.: Banner of Truth, 1999), 18.
8. Watson, *Doctrine of Repentance*, 18–58.
9. Tim Chester, *You Can Change: God's Transforming Power for Our Sinful Behavior and Negative Emotions* (Wheaton, Ill.: Crossway, 2010), 73.
10. Ibid., 73–98.
11. Steven Curtis Chapman and Scotty Smith, *Restoring Broken Things* (Nashville: Nelson, 2007), 105.
12. Timothy S. Lane and Paul David Tripp, *How People Change* (Greensboro, N.C.: New Growth Press, 2008), 6.

CHAPTER 5

1. Bruce McNichol, quoted in "Churches Die with Dignity," *Christianity Today* (January 14, 1991), 69.
2. Robert E. Coleman, *The Master Plan of Evangelism*, 3rd ed. (Grand Rapids: Baker, 2006), 18, 21.
3. Bryan Chapell, *Holiness by Grace* (Wheaton, Ill.: Crossway, 2001), 154.
4. Names withheld. Used by permission.
5. Mark Hall, "Slow Fade," Copyright © 2007 Club Zoo Music (BMI).
6. Paul David Tripp, *Instruments in the Redeemer's Hands* (Phillipsburg, N.J.: P&R, 2002), 54.
7. Os Guinness, *The Call: Finding and Fulfilling the Central Purpose of Your Life* (Nashville: W, 2003), 4.
8. Ibid., 20.
9. Adapted from J. Allen Thompson, *Coaching Urban Church Planters* (New York: Redeemer Church, 2005), 53, 56.

10. Martin Luther, *A Commentary on St. Paul's Epistle to the Galatians* (Philadelphia: Smith, English, & Co., 1860), 206.

CHAPTER 6

1. Timothy S. Laniak, *Shepherds after My Own Heart* (Downers Grove, Ill.: InterVarsity, 2006), 18.
2. S. David Moore, *The Shepherding Movement Controversy and Charismatic Ecclesiology* (New York: T&T Clark, 2003) 196.
3. The word *charge* in 1 Peter 5:3 translates a Greek word (*klēros*) that means an allotment of land. It refers to the allotted portion or inheritance; specifically one's possession or what is possessed. "In 1 Pt 5:3 the *klēroi* seem to denote the 'flock' as a whole, i.e. the various parts of the people of God which have been assigned as 'portions' to individual elders or shepherds (of the various portions that combine to form a whole …)" (F. W. Danker, ed. *A Greek-English Lexicon of the New Testament and Other Early Christian Literature*, 3rd ed. [Chicago: University of Chicago Press, 2000], 548).

CHAPTER 7

1. John Wooden and Don Yeager, *A Game Plan for Life: The Power of Mentoring* (New York: Bloomsbury, 2009), 3–5.
2. See David Peterson, *Engaging with God: A Biblical Theology of Worship* (Downers Grove, Ill.: InterVarsity, 1992), 67.
3. See H. R. P. Dickson, *The Arab of the Desert* (London: Allen & Unwin, 1949), 402–403; see also Jeremiah 33:13.
4. Timothy Z. Witmer, *The Shepherd Leader* (Phillipsburg, N.J.: P&R, 2010), 109.
5. Edward G. Selwyn, *The First Epistle of Peter* (Grand Rapids: Baker, 1981), 231.
6. Timothy S. Laniak, *Shepherds after My Own Heart* (Downers Grove, Ill.: InterVarsity, 2006), 234.
7. See Bob Logan, *Coaching 101 Handbook* (St. Charles, Ill.: ChurchSmart, 2003).
8. Richard Baxter, *Reformed Pastor* (1656; repr., Carlisle, Pa.: Banner of Truth, 1997), 91.

CHAPTER 8

1. Simon Kistemaker, *Peter and John* (Grand Rapids: Baker, 1987), 194.
2. Timothy Laniak, *While Shepherds Watch Their Flocks* (Matthews, N.C.: ShepherdLeader Publications, 2007), 59.
3. John Calvin, *Commentaries*, trans. John Owens (Grand Rapids: Baker, 1984), 22:144.
4. Paul D. Stanley and J. Robert Clinton, *Connecting: The Mentoring Relationships You Need to Succeed in Life* (Colorado Springs: NavPress, 1992), 78.

CHAPTER 9

1. Timothy Z. Witmer, *The Shepherd Leader* (Phillipsburg, N.J.: P&R, 2010), 156.
2. Tim Pollard, *The Leadership Opportunity* (Billings, Mont.: Peacemaker Ministries, 2009), 55–71. Used by permission.

CHAPTER 10

1. Associated Press, "450 Turkish Sheep Leap to Their Deaths," July 8, 2005, www.foxnews.com/story/0,2933,161949,00.html (accessed July 2, 2010).
2. Dietrich Bonhoeffer, *Life Together: The Classic Exploration of Christian Community* (New York: Harper, 1978), 97.
3. Sam Crabtree, *Practicing Affirmation* (Wheaton, Ill.: Crossway, 2011), 64–71.

CHAPTER 11

1. Michael Coggin, "Listening for Life: Picking Up on Verbal and Nonverbal Signals," http://theresurgence.com/files/pdf/michael_coggin_2005_listening_for_life.pdf (accessed November 29, 2011).
2. Adapted from MindTools, "Active Listening: Hear What People Are Really Saying,"

http://www.mindtools.com/CommSkll/ActiveListening.htm (accessed November 29, 2011).

3. C. S. Lewis, *Mere Christianity* (New York: Macmillan, 1981), 190.

4. Tim Keller, "Vocation: Three Parts to Discerning a Call" (Q & A Session; New York: Redeemer Presbyterian Resources), www.redeemer.com/learn/resources/resources/Vocation-Three_parts_to_discerning_a_call.m3u.

5. Charles E. Hummel, *The Tyranny of the Urgent*, rev. ed. (Downers Grove, Ill.: Inter-Varsity, 1994), 5–6.

CHAPTER 12

1. Elyse Fitzpatrick and Dennis E. Johnson, *Counsel from the Cross* (Wheaton, Ill: Crossway, 2009), 12.

2. Robert E. Logan, *Coaching 101: Discover the Power of Coaching* (St. Charles, Ill: Church Smart Resources, 2003), 14.

3. Paul D. Stanley and J. Robert Clinton, *Connecting: The Mentoring Relationships You Need to Succeed in Life* (Colorado Springs: NavPress, 1992), 76.

4. Kenneth Blanchard, *The Heart of a Leader* (Tulsa, Okla.: Libri, 1998), 15.

5. J. I. Packer, *Keep in Step with the Spirit* (Grand Rapids: Baker, 1984), 66.

6. Steve Brown, *When Being Good Isn't Good Enough* (Nashville: Nelson, 1990), 28.

7. Robert K. Flayhart, "Gospel-Centered Mentoring" (DMin diss., Covenant Theological Seminary, 2002), 212. Flayhart uses other terms and ordering to describe his gospel waltz: "repentance, faith, and fight."

8. Martin Luther, *Galatians*, ed. Alister McGrath and J. I. Packer (Wheaton, Ill.: Crossway, 1998), xx–xxi.

9. We recommend Peacemaker Ministries (www.peacemaker.net) and their valuable resources for further understanding on this important subject.

CHAPTER 13

1. Richard P. Kaufmann, "The Gospel-Driven Church" (unpublished lecture notes), based on Harbor Presbyterian's core value #1.

RE:LIT

Tools for training

Millions of Christians around the world come to the Resurgence for training. Our mission is to help you on the mission God has given you.

Re:Lit is the publishing arm of the Resurgence. We provide books specifically designed to communicate essential truths about God and life. Since real change begins in the heart, we concentrate on heart-level issues like worship vs. idolatry, love vs. hate, and gospel freedom vs. sin's slavery. We believe Christians need both repentant hearts and solid theology so that they can do the work God has called them to. We provide the tools you need to put knowledge and passion into effective action and walk in the good works to which God has called you.

FOR A FULL LIST OF OUR BOOKS, OR TO LEARN MORE ABOUT THE RESURGENCE, VISIT *RELIT.ORG*.